Selma Lagerlöf

Twayne's World Authors Series

Scandinavian Literature

Leif Sjöberg, Editor

State University of New York at Stony Brook

TWAS 741

SELMA LAGERLÖF
Drawing by Oskar Kokoschka, 1917
Photograph courtesy of Svenska porträttarkivet,
Nationalmuseum, Stockholm

Selma Lagerlöf

By Vivi Edström
University of Stockholm

Translated by Barbara Lide
Michigan Technological University

Twayne Publishers • *Boston*

Selma Lagerlöf

Vivi Edström
Translated by Barbara Lide

Copyright © 1984 by G. K. Hall & Company
All Rights Reserved
Published by Twayne Publishers
A Division of G. K. Hall & Company
70 Lincoln Street
Boston, Massachusetts 02111

Book Production by Elizabeth Todesco

Book Design by Barbara Anderson

Printed on permanent/durable acid-free
paper and bound in the United States of
America.

Library of Congress Cataloging in Publication Data

Edström, Vivi Blom, 1923–
  Selma Lagerlöf.

  (Twayne's world authors series; TWAS 741.
Scandinavian literature)
  Bibliography: p. 142
  Includes index.
  1. Lagerlöf, Selma, 1858–1950—
Criticism and interpretation.   I. Title.
II. Series: Twayne's world authors series; TWAS 741.
III. Series: Twayne's world authors series. Scandinavian literature.
PT9771.E3   1984   839.7'372   84–6749
ISBN 0–8057–6587–5

Contents

About the Author

Vivi Edström is a professor of literature, especially children's literature, at the University of Stockholm. She received her doctorate from the University of Gothenburg with a dissertation on the structure of *Gösta Berling's Saga* by Selma Lagerlöf: *Livets stigar: Tiden, handlingen och livskänslan i Gösta Berlings saga* (The roads of life: Time, action, and vital forces in Gösta Berling's saga, 1960). She is president of the Selma Lagerlöf Society and is the author of several articles about this writer. In 1980 she published a study on narrative art in children's books: *Barnbokens form: En studie i konsten att berätta* (Form in childrens' books: A study in narrative art). She has edited *Ungdomsboken—mönster och värderingar* (The junior book—evaluations and patterns, 1984) and has written numerous articles on children's literature.

Preface

Selma Lagerlöf (1858–1940) was born in a modest country manor called Mårbacka in the district of Värmland, a Swedish province with a strong literary tradition. Her writing brought her fame as well as wealth; it enabled her, when she was in her fifties, to establish herself as owner of Mårbacka and rebuild the estate of her ancestors. While she took an active interest in the agricultural affairs of her estate, she remained passionately committed to her calling as a writer.

Lagerlöf and her literary works have been the subjects of extensive research, both in Sweden and, to some measure, in countries outside Sweden. Early in her career, she became just as popular in Germany as she was in her homeland; indeed, the first significant monograph on Lagerlöf was published in German by Walter Berendsohn as early as 1927, an abridged version of which was translated into both Swedish and English. In the English-speaking world, her works did not attain the popularity that they had in Central Europe; in America, however, her books were received with greater enthusiasm than in England. Lagerlöf herself expressed her admiration for America, "the great daughterland in the West," in a radio speech directed at America in 1933. For her, it was a country that afforded the possibility for the development of a new civilization and a new humanity.

In 1942 the Swedish novelist Elin Wägner published a monograph that presents a wealth of information about Lagerlöf's literary works, as well as a fascinating picture of the unrest and searching behind her calm façade. Beginning in the late 1950s, and for ten years thereafter, a series of doctoral dissertations and major critical studies appeared in print, which examine in detail virtually all of Lagerlöf's works. The Selma Lagerlöf Society was established in 1958. Since its founding it has published essays and other studies devoted exclusively to Lagerlöf and her literary works. All of these factors have contributed to the creation of a many-faceted picture of Lagerlöf, her environment, and her literary oeuvre. Yet certain aspects of her work still have not been treated by scholars. To this date Lagerlöf research has been predominantly analytical, biographical, and, to a certain extent, ideological. The older conception of Lagerlöf as a simple teller of tales has become more complex. But much work remains to be done, especially in connection with the relationship between her literary works and the symbolist movement, which reached its peak around the turn of the century. Nor has a complete study been made of the psychological aspects of her stories, despite a long awareness of her deep insight into human nature. The study at hand emphasizes character depiction and points out the symbolic language that Lagerlöf uses in delineating her characters. One of its aims is to contribute to the understanding of the psychological aspects of Lagerlöf's works.

Another important area relatively untapped in Lagerlöf research is the reception and impact of her books, both in Sweden and abroad. Studying Lagerlöf as a female author also provides an interesting perspective. This role has been highlighted in the introduction to an American translation of her short novel *Herr Arnes penningar (The Treasure)*, brought out by an American feminist press. The present study also calls attention to the female point of view in her stories.

This book is organized as a series of monographic chapters centering on her work. This seemed to be the most natural arrangement, since Lagerlöf's narratives appear as worlds enclosed in themselves, each with its own distinctive character. The most thorough analysis is devoted to *Gösta Berling's Saga*, her debut novel and a work regarded by many as her most remarkable book. In *The Epic Tradition in "Gösta Berling's Saga,"* the American scholar Elsa Olson-Buckner places this novel within the tradition of the epics of world literature. *Gösta Berling's Saga* also embodies a good many of the lyric and romantic qualities that characterize the literature of the 1890s in the North.

Although her next major novel, *Jerusalem* (1901–2), shares certain similarities of organization, structure, and plot with *Gösta Berling's Saga*, it is essentially a different kind of novel, a monumental two-volume work of epic proportions, narrated in a restrained manner that contrasts sharply with the vividly lyrical, and occasionally exuberant, style of *Gösta Berling's Saga*.

The best known of all Lagerlöf's works is undoubtedly the book she originally wrote for Swedish school children, *The Wonderful Adventures of Nils (Nils Holgerssons underbara resa genom Sverige)*, which has been translated into more than forty languages. Her legends, however, are her most important contribution to world literature.

Lagerlöf also wrote a considerable number of short stories, as well as splendid short novels, one of which, *The Treasure,* is treated in this book.

Lagerlöf was a highly prolific writer who continued to produce works of literary significance well into her late years. In her memoirs, she uses a narrative technique reminiscent of Proust as she reaches back to an irrevocably lost past. Her literary career concludes with a genealogical trilogy, *The Ring of the Löwenskölds (Löwensköldska ringen, Charlotte Löwensköld, Anna Svärd,)* in which she displays the great range of her psychological insight and the whole register of her narrative virtuosity.

Despite spending decades of her life in the public eye, Lagerlöf was a rather introverted and withdrawn person. The concluding chapter discusses her in the role of writer, her views of herself as an observer of life, and her early ambition to become a popular author. Finally, mention is made of the myths surrounding her, both personally and as a writer, that have been created by critics, scholars, and readers.

Although Lagerlöf's works exhibit a good deal of formal and thematic variety—much more than people usually give her credit for—they also have a strong thread of continuity. Lagerlöf always returns, for example, to the basic questions of human values and the risks of existence. The moral perspective, too, is always present in her work.

She often found material for her stories in folktales, fairy tales, and legends. But her interpretation and her own rendering of these simple stories are complex; her narratives are sharply realistic, and at the same time symbolic and mythical. It is with this complexity of Lagerlöf's vision that this study is primarily concerned.

Vivi Edström

University of Stockholm

Chronology

1907   Purchases Mårbacka, the home of her childhood.

1908   *En saga om en saga* (*The Girl from the Marshcroft*), collection of short stories.

1909   Wins Nobel Prize for literature.

1910   Purchases the entire Mårbacka estate and becomes an active landowner.

1911   *Liljecronas hem* (*Liliecrona's Home*), novel. Delivers her speech "Home and State" at the International Congress on Women's Suffrage.

1912   *Körkarlen* (*Thy Soul Shall Bear Witness*), novel. Travel in Finland and Russia.

1914   *Kejsarn av Portugallien* (*The Emperor of Portugallia*), novel. Becomes a member of the Swedish Academy.

1915   *Troll och människor 1* (*Trolls and Men*, 1), collection of stories and short prose. Mother dies.

1918   *Bannlyst* (*The Outcast*), novel.

1920   *Zachris Topelius*, monograph on the Finno-Swedish writer.

1921   *Troll och människor 2* (*Trolls and Men*, 2). Sophie Elkan dies.

1922   *Mårbacka*, first part of her memoirs.

1925   *Löwensköldska ringen* (*The General's Ring*) and *Charlotte Löwensköld*, first two volumes of the Löwensköld trilogy.

1928   *Anna Svärd*, final volume of *The Ring of the Löwenskölds, a Trilogy*.

1930   *Ett barns memoarer* (*Memories of My Childhood*).

1932   *Dagbok för Selma Ottilia Lovisa Lagerlöf* (*The Diary of Selma Lagerlöf*).

1933   *Höst* (*Harvest*), collection of short prose. Edition of her complete works.

1940   Dies 16 March at Mårbacka.

Chapter One
Biographical Perspective
The Girl Who Won World Fame

Selma Lagerlöf is usually described as a plain, ordinary girl who almost miraculously came to be regarded with the highest possible esteem. She began her career as a writer in a simple attic flat in Landskrona, a city in the south of Sweden, where she was earning her living as a teacher. That is where she wrote her first important novel, *Gösta Berling's Saga.* Her breakthrough, however, did not come overnight. Her fame rose slowly but surely from the 1890s on, culminating with her winning the Nobel Prize for Literature in 1909.

Lagerlöf lived a rich and interesting life, filled with creative work, critical success, and much public acclaim both at home and abroad. While her literary works are rooted in the nature and traditions of her native land, her art is nonetheless universal. Like many novelists before her, she appealed not only to the literary world but to a broader reading public as well. It was she who taught Swedes to read, with *The Wonderful Adventures of Nils,* a book about the geography of Sweden written for schoolchildren.

Lagerlöf became a widely loved and respected author. Her home Mårbacka, in the west-central province of Värmland, remains, as it was during her lifetime, a mecca for her admirers. Unfortunately, there are two sides to success. For Lagerlöf it brought with it impudent tourists, beggars, and all manner of requests for help. She gradually became an institution, asked to take a stand on contemporary questions and to express herself on all matters. People placed unreasonable demands upon her, expecting her, as a writer, to act as a social conscience. But she herself often took the initiative, coming forward and making known her opinions. This she did, for example, at the Universal Christian Conference on Life and Work— a major ecumenical conference held in Stockholm in 1925. She also was a willing participant in the struggle for women's suffrage. Eventually her name was placed among the ranks of famous Swedish women: St. Birgitta, Queen Christina, Fredrika Bremer, and Ellen Key. Her accomplishments as a feminist will be discussed in the concluding chapter.

Her life can indeed be described as a saga. But even a saga usually has a rational basis. One explanation for Lagerlöf's exceptional success is her talent—a combination of self-assured strength of will and a bold creative imagination. The Swedish novelist Elin Wägner characterizes this talent aptly in her sympathetic biography of her great predecessor: "Selma Lagerlöf had an expansive soul that desired to burst all constraints, irrespective of where its powers took her."[1] The environment in which Lagerlöf grew up was especially favorable for a budding writer. Värmland is the mystical region of Swedish literature, where the literary culture enjoys a special symbiotic relationship with the beautiful countryside. Many poets and writers of Värmland—among them Erik Gustaf Geijer, Esaias Tegnér, Gustaf Fröding, Tage Aurell, Göran Tunström, and, of course, Lagerlöf herself—possess a singular combination of an ability to fantasize and fabricate with a talent for achieving verisimilitude.

Lagerlöf's dream of becoming a writer began in her childhood home, Mårbacka, a modest family estate in the parish of East Ämtervik in the heart of Värmland. Life there followed a certain cultural standard set by the higher classes of the day. In the evenings, classic works of literature were read aloud. People made music and told stories, engaged in skits and amateur theatrics. It was an environment that helped develop the imagination of a receptive child. Lagerlöf's roots in her native soil were her most important source of inspiration, and she constantly returned to material from Värmland and "Svartsjö," as she called her home parish in her stories. Even when a certain motif belonged to a foreign milieu, she often placed the story in Värmland, at the center of which was the original Mårbacka, with its low houses, its carp pond, its apple trees, and its roses.

Childhood

Selma Lagerlöf was next to the youngest in a family of five children, two sons and three daughters. Others who lived with the family were an Aunt Lovisa, who figures in Lagerlöf's Mårbacka books, a housekeeper, a governess, maids, and farmhands. There was also a beloved grandmother who told stories to the children and

who died when Selma was five. Though they had been members of
the landed gentry since the seventeenth century, the Lagerlöfs found
their position slipping in the face of growing economic problems.

Lagerlöf has written about her family and her childhood in a series
of three books, the first of which is entitled, simply, *Mårbacka*. It
was published in 1922, but the preparatory work had been under
way for more than ten years. The other two books are *Memories of
My Childhood* (1930) and *The Diary of Selma Lagerlöf* (1932). Although the Mårbacka books deal with the development of Lagerlöf
as a writer, they are also about the soil on which the gifted girl
grew up. The first centers on the manor itself—its history, which
becomes a blend of fact and legend, its people, and its everyday
life. Lagerlöf fondly remembers "the never-failing tenderness" she
encountered in her childhood. She also presents a dramatic account
of the paralysis that struck her at the age of three, making it
impossible for her to walk. The paralysis was cured, but Lagerlöf—
who so often and so enthusiastically described the joys of the dance—
walked with a limp for the rest of her life. In the chapter, "The
Bird of Paradise," she tells of how she suddenly regained the ability
to walk one day when she was on a boat and was shown a magnificent
stuffed bird. The story of how experiencing something so beautiful
made her paralysis disappear suggests a psychological reason for her
illness.

The concern over not being able to move like others is expressed—
with greater and lesser degrees of disguise—in her memoirs, but
nowhere is it as predominant as in the chapter "The Ball at Sunne"
in *Memories of My Childhood*. When Selma is about thirteen, her
father forces her to attend a dance at a manor. The other girls are
full of expectation, but Selma cries. Certain that she will not be
asked to dance, she beseeches her father to let her stay home, but
her father, whose will is the law of the family, disregards her fears.
The story, however, has an optimistic conclusion, with the father
suddenly deciding that his daughter should be allowed to go to
Stockholm and receive treatment for her leg.

The Diary of Selma Lagerlöf, third in the series of memoirs, deals
with her visit to Stockholm in 1873, when she was fourteen. The
book presents both an exquisite picture of the times and an account
of a teenager's dreams and fantasies of love. Selma meets a young
student, around whom she weaves a romantic fantasy. This gives
an autobiographical cast to many of the love fantasies found in her

stories. While the *Diary* is a subtle depiction of a teenaged girl's
identity crisis, it also shows the development of a budding writer,
a young person with an unusual talent for observation, who registers
all that she sees around her and then combines it into a rich blend
of the experienced and the imagined.

The style in the *Diary* assumes the level of the young first-person
narrator so perfectly that one critic believed that Lagerlöf had published her very own diary from her teens. He remarked that an adult
writer could not write in such a vigorous and direct manner—an
assertion that amused Lagerlöf considerably, since the diary is a
work purely of her imagination. She was over seventy when she so
accurately re-created the thoughts and feelings of a fourteen-year-
old.[2]

Although there was a tradition of love for literature in Lagerlöf's
family, her parents had no special talents along literary lines. As is
frequently the case with girls who are intellectually inclined, the
father seems to have had the greater importance for her, and she
was eager to win his affection and admiration. Lieutenant Erik
Gustaf Lagerlöf was apparently a problematic person with a despotic
streak. The father-daughter relationship is an emotion-charged theme
in Lagerlöf's works. The main character in her memoirs, her father
is presented as an engaging man who charmed those around him.
Every year people came to Mårbacka from all over the district to
celebrate his birthday, which became a festival of games, play acting,
dancing, singing, and music making.

Family and social life as portrayed in the Mårbacka books are
sometimes reminiscent of the provincial life depicted in Turgenev
and Chekhov or in Proust. But, as was the case in both Russia and
France, the idyll was only an illusion. The social conditions in
Sweden were not as complicated as those in larger countries that
experienced major revolutionary upheavals, but even in Sweden a
new era was knocking at the door. During the 1860s and 1870s,
economic conditions in Värmland were deteriorating in a manner
that was devastating for the traditional social order of manor house
and farm. Agricultural prices sank, and the iron industry—the most
important of the region—was threatened. At first the large foundries
suffered, but gradually the smaller landed estates such as Mårbacka
were also affected. It was difficult for the Lagerlöfs to manage,
despite the fact that the mother came from a well-established, wealthy
family. She was taciturn and somewhat colorless, but she provided

the family with a stable point in their uneasy existence. The father had grandiose ideas for developing the estate, but by and large he was unsuccessful in his undertakings. As it became more and more difficult for him to endure the stress, he took to drink and fell sick. He died in 1885. Three years later, Mårbacka had to be sold and the household goods auctioned off. One of the sons, Johan, emigrated to America.

The years in the family's history that led to this most severe blow—the loss of her childhood home—are not described by Lagerlöf in her memoirs. In the chapter entitled "The Earthquake" in *Memories of My Childhood,* however, she invokes the devastation of a natural catastrophe in order to recall the fear brought about by the crisis that threatened her home. She had planned to follow up "The Earthquake" with a narrative about the years of adversity, but she did not carry out her intentions. Perhaps the task seemed too painful. She used the excuse that she did not want to bore her readers with sorrowful things.[3] In her strictly fictional works, on the other hand, she re-creates her shattering experience in different ways. The risk of losing a beloved estate is a recurring theme in her work, with the motif of the auction presented in an especially empathetic manner, both in *Gösta Berling's Saga* and *Jerusalem.* There may be several reasons for Lagerlöf's failure to depict her family's crisis, one of which could be that the tone she had chosen for her autobiographical books was an idyllic one that prevented her from examining too closely the unhappy experiences of her life.

The value of memoirs as biographical source material is, of course, always doubtful. The Dutch scholar Stine de Vrieze, in a study entitled "Fact and Fiction in the Autobiographical World of Selma Lagerlöf," has shown how Lagerlöf uses a number of fictionalizing tricks to make her books at the same time more dramatic and more harmonious than the reality actually was. She compares Lagerlöf's narrative method with that of Goethe's *Dichtung und Wahrheit (Poetry and Truth),* Hans Christian Andersen's *Mit Livs Eventyr (The True Fairy Tale of My Life),* and Proust's *À la recherche du temps perdu (Remembrance of Things Past).* But the Mårbacka books are most closely related to *Dichtung und Wahrheit;* in both cases, one can speak of a "harmonious realism." Like Goethe, Lagerlöf places herself in the background, allowing her narrative to be dominated by the setting and the persons that inhabit it. Also like Goethe, she works with seemingly naive devices and indulgent humor, placing the stress on the intimate history of the immediate family and relatives, the culture, and the friendly, intimate atmosphere. The perspective of distance in time allows for embellishing reality. The actual problems are touched with a light hand, but the sensitive reader can perceive them under the harmonious surface.[4]

At the time Lagerlöf was writing her memoirs, Proust's *Remembrance of Things Past* had begun to be recognized and read outside of France. In a letter written when she was working on the third book of the Mårbacka series, she reflects on Proust's method of depicting his childhood through the eyes of a child with the temperament of an adult. She found the technique unusual and apparently was fascinated by it.[5] In certain places in the Mårbacka books, she approaches her own recollections in a manner reminiscent of Proust's. In one instance, a cherished little bookmark calls forth a whole succession of smells, colors, and visual pictures from the past. Proust's complicated interplay between the child and the adults, in which the adults reveal how insensitive they are to the child's fears, corresponds to passages in Lagerlöf—for example, in the abovementioned story of the painful experience concerning the ball at Sunne. Like Proust's Marcel, Selma tries in vain to get an adult to understand and be considerate of her feelings.

Education

Lagerlöf's education began at Mårbacka with governesses who in some cases became family friends and were important for her development. Languages, literature, music, and history were considered fitting subjects for the children to learn at home. The sons were later sent to schools and to the university, which, of course, put a strain on the family finances. The oldest daughter, Anna, married young and bore a child, but both she and the child died early. Their deaths were clearly a tragedy for the family, but Lagerlöf never touches upon the subject directly in her literary works. The other two daughters, Gerda and Selma, remained at home. Selma took over the role of governess, with the task of instructing her rather recalcitrant sister. In some of the unpublished outlines for the memoirs, she describes the young girls' existence on the remote estate as uneventful and gloomy—a picture that did not fit into the harmonious pattern of the books and therefore was not included.[6]

As a consequence of the family's declining fortunes after 1875, the sisters' prospects for the future became dimmer. Their lives seemed to have alternated between expectant optimism and resignation. The role of daughters living at home was an empty one for them, since they were not involved in any productive or meaningful work. Selma was not only uninterested in household activities; she was awkward in the kitchen and not at all good at sewing and embroidery, activities regarded as proper for girls of her social class.[7] Like so many other girls in her situation, what she had to look forward to was a life as a governess or lady's companion, for one could not count on a suitable proposal of marriage. With a touch of gallows humor, the nineteen-year-old Selma described herself and her sister as being "kind-hearted but hardly pretty."[8] Early photographs of her show a face with intelligent, well-defined features, with something especially captivating about the eyes. But as her biographer Elin Wägner pointedly remarks, her unusual eyes were not discovered until she had become famous.[9]

The picture presented here of Selma Lagerlöf's youth is perhaps far too dark. Despite everything, she created a not unhappy world of her own that revolved around her reading and studies, becoming thereby considerably well read at an early age. From childhood on, she seemed to have been certain of her calling as a writer, with her dreams first nourished by listening to stories at Mårbacka, where the tradition of oral narrative was very much alive. Her Aunt Nana, often mentioned in her works, was a brilliant storyteller. The family reading sessions acquainted the children with literary classics as well as folktales; the works of Shakespeare, Byron, and Goethe were read, along with those of the Swedish romantic writers. A good deal of popular literature was also read at Mårbacka, through which Lagerlöf acquired a taste for long, exciting novels with complicated intrigues, such as those of Wilkie Collins, Eugenie Marlitt—a German writer of women's fiction—and Alexandre Dumas père. The first book that instilled in her a desire to become a novelist was *Oceola*—a story about Indians by Mayne Reid, a British novelist who had spent some time in the American West—which she read when she was seven. As a teenager, she came to idolize Walter Scott. Also among her favorite reading was *Heimskringla: The History of the Kings of Norway* by Snorri Sturluson, the great Icelandic historian of the Middle Ages.

There are traces of all this reading in her works. In the short narrative entitled "A Saga about a Saga," she tells of her first attempt at writing: "When she tried to write, she chose material from her books and cheerfully put together stories about the sultans of *A Thousand and One Nights,* the knights of Walter Scott, and the legendary kings of Snorri Sturluson."

Her earliest attempts at writing were not stories but occasional poems. The next step on her path to becoming an author were the puppet plays that she wrote in a romantic style occasionally bordering on parody, and which were performed in an attic at Mårbacka from 1877 to 1888, when she was around nineteen or twenty years old.[10]

Lagerlöf had the good fortune of having her talent as a writer discovered by an enthusiastic and influential person. In 1880, the twenty-two-year-old Selma was a bridesmaid at a wedding at which she recited a poem she had written for the occasion. Among the guests was a woman named Eva Fryxell, an ardent advocate of feminism who, like so many other feminists of her day, directed many of her efforts toward seeking out talented women. Fryxell encouraged Lagerlöf to pursue a formal education. Despite her family's shaky financial situation and her father's opposition, she managed to borrow money and made her way to Stockholm, where, after completing some supplementary courses, she was admitted to the Higher Teacher's College for Women, in its day a "university" for gifted young women. Lagerlöf has described the happiness she felt at the news that she had passed her entrance examination.[11] For her it meant that the door to a new life had been opened, and she could escape her seeming fate; she would not need to seek a position as a governess or a lady's companion in a strange family. Undoubtedly the painful departure from her family home was most decisive for her future. Had she stayed at Mårbacka, she probably would have remained a village genius with few possibilities for development.

Lagerlöf has described her years in Stockholm (1881–85) as a period of "awakening, growth, and rapid maturation."[12] She was older than most of the women in her class, self-possessed, and taciturn, and her companions regarded her as clever and mature. While her major interests were literature and history, she also showed an enthusiasm for the natural sciences. She wrote much poetry; during one period she experienced a veritable "sonnet fever" and dreamed of becoming Sweden's greatest poet.

But there was more to her life than school. Lagerlöf seized the opportunity to participate in the active cultural life of Stockholm, primarily the opera and theater. She gave form to her experiences in a series of sonnets portraying figures from the stage—Don Juan, Falstaff, Mary Stuart, and Mephistopheles. *Faust* was especially significant for her. When she was younger, she had read Goethe's drama; now, in Stockholm, she experienced *Faust* as an opera and wrote no less than five sonnets about the figures in both Gounod's *Faust* and Boito's *Mefistofele*. One can see traces of *Faust* in her first novel. *Gösta Berling's Saga* is based on a contract with Sintram, who is the counterpart of Mephisto, although Lagerlöf's devil is of a more folkloric type.[13] Hjalmar Gullberg, Lagerlöf's successor as a member of the Swedish Academy, made an accurate observation when he characterized the theater sonnets as literary costume sketches for the cavaliers and beautiful ladies in *Gösta Berling's Saga*.[14]

The most important experience of Lagerlöf's years in Stockholm was her inspiration for that great novel. In "A Saga about a Saga," she relates that she was walking down a street in Stockholm when it suddenly occurred to her that she possessed a unique source of material in her memories of home. Stories and anecdotes about the eccentric people of Värmland ought to provide material as captivating as that used by Carl Michael Bellman (1740–95) and Johan Ludvig Runeberg (1804–77)—whose poems are among the most highly acclaimed in the Swedish language—when they wrote about persons they knew. The inspiration was so overpowering that the street seemed to sway under her feet. Before she could realize her plans, however, she had to find a position that would enable her to pay off the loan she had taken out in order to be able to complete her studies.

The Teacher

Shortly after her father died in 1885, Lagerlöf, dressed in mourning, took over her first and only post as a teacher. It was a position at a school for girls in Landskrona, a small city in southwestern Sweden on the shores of Öresund, a short distance by sea from Copenhagen, which, with its cultural life, offered a stimulating change from the small-town existence that Lagerlöf described with the words "we sleep very very soundly."[15]

It was in Landskrona, however, that she experienced the first stirrings of a strong social commitment. She was also interested in pedagogical matters. As she wrote in one of her later stories, she was generally involved in everything "that concerned teaching, peace,

temperance, feminism, and care of the poor."[16] She also participated
in the social life the city offered and acquired close friends among
her colleagues, all of whom were women.

In this period of her development, Lagerlöf experienced trying
personal problems. The departure from her childhood home had
been a bitter experience, but leaving Mårbacka apparently stimulated her dreams of becoming a writer. If it is true that a great
sorrow can inspire artistic creativity, then that is the case in the
creation of her first book. *Gösta Berling's Saga* grew out of loss and
longing, as Lagerlöf herself pointed out in a letter:

> They say that a great sorrow or a deep loss is necessary to teach a person
> to write, and I experienced such a thing when my old, dear home had to
> be sold a few years ago. It has been since then that I taught myself to
> write, to throw myself, with my sorrow and joy, into my work. And in
> one way or another, this book has, so to speak, returned my home to
> me.[17]

Separated from her home, Lagerlöf now was able to gain an important
perspective on her original milieu. She points out in "A Saga about
a Saga" that the loss of her childhood home actually had occasioned
Gösta Berling's Saga and that she had written the book in order to
"save for herself what she still might be able to save of her home:
the beloved old stories, the pleasant peace of the carefree days, and
the beautiful landscape with its long lakes and blue hills."

In 1890, Lagerlöf achieved an important success by winning first
prize in a literary contest sponsored by the women's journal *Idun*.
She had submitted five chapters of *Gösta Berling's Saga*. These were
then printed in a separate edition and received favorable reviews.
Winning the prize boosted her self-confidence, and she took a leave
of absence from school and completed her first major novel, which
came out around Christmas of 1891.

The Author

Lagerlöf had hoped that her first novel would be such a success
that she would be able to give up teaching and make her living as
a writer, but these hopes were not to be realized until 1895. As a
completed work, *Gösta Berling's Saga* was received with a lack of
understanding and negative criticism. Misunderstanding the nature
of the book completely, several reviewers judged it by narrow re-

alistic criteria.[18] It was only after the highly respected Danish critic Georg Brandes wrote a positive review of the novel that it gained acclaim in Sweden. That was in 1893, two years after its publication. The next year, Lagerlöf published a collection of short stories entitled *Osynliga länkar (Invisible Links)*, which was an undisputed success. She was now recognized as a writer of short stories and sought after as a contributor to several journals.

In 1895, she received a traveling stipend from King Oscar II, which enabled her to break out of the narrow confines of her existence. She used her stipend money to travel to Italy, where she spent several months (October 1895–May 1896). On this, her first trip abroad, she devoted less time to pleasure than to work. She was interested in both the history and mythology of Italy, as well as its contemporary social problems. The immediate result of the journey was the 1897 novel *Antikrists mirakler (The Miracles of Antichrist)*, which contains an extraordinary depiction of Sicily and southern Italy.

Not long after returning from Italy, Lagerlöf moved to the city of Falun in Dalecarlia, a district northeast of Värmland, close to where her younger sister Gerda lived with her family. With royalties beginning to flow in, she was able to settle down comfortably as a successful writer. Dalecarlia provided new inspiration for her writing. It is a region where the peasantry—representatives of old Swedish independence and strength—has always been of great importance. Dalecarlia is usually regarded as a Sweden in miniature, with its extensive woodlands, numerous lakes, and genuine folk culture, which includes colorful traditional folk costumes, fiddle music, and the well-known Dalecarlian folk paintings. It provided the setting for Lagerlöf's next major novel, *Jerusalem,* a work that tells of a religious revival that takes place among a group of farmers who leave Sweden to settle in the Holy Land.[19]

From her move to Dalecarlia until the outbreak of World War I, Lagerlöf enjoyed an extremely productive period. She wrote her important book for children, *Nils Holgerssons underbara resa genom Sverige (The Wonderful Adventures of Nils)*. She published several short novels, among them the notable expressionistic story, *Körkarlen (Thy Soul Shall Bear Witness)*. After the turn of the century, Lagerlöf reached the peak of her fame, receiving in 1907 an honorary doctoral degree from the University of Uppsala and in 1909 the Nobel Prize for Literature. When she made a journey to Finland and Russia in

1912, she was widely lionized. In 1914 she was elected to the
Swedish Academy—the first woman to receive this honor. It was
perhaps still more important for her personal life, however, that she
was able to establish herself as the owner of her old family estate.
When in 1908 she received an offer to buy back the house at
Mårbacka, she did not hesitate. Later, with her Nobel Prize money,
she also purchased the land around the manor house. Now an old
wish of hers had been fulfilled—to own a farm.

The Lady of the Manor

Energetic and enterprising in the management of her lands, Lagerlöf still was unable to keep from being affected by the poor economic conditions in the 1920s and 1930s. After making substantial
improvements and investments in farm equipment, she realized that
all her efforts to make the estate profitable had not succeeded.[20] She
did, however, create a sensation when she began the production of
Mårbacka oatmeal.

Lagerlöf exhibited a matriarchal interest in those who worked on
the estate, in her cows and other farm animals, and in the crops
and produce. In her notebooks from the later years at Mårbacka,
information about her literary works alternates with figures for the
income on the sale of pigs and for farm expenses, revealing that her
thoughts were divided between the search for new insights into
human possibilities and practical matters of running the estate. She
also took part in affairs of the parish and supported important
enterprises in the district. Her father's ambitious plans were now
realized by his daughter. Mårbacka, which had been a cozy, unpretentious house, was transformed into a magnificent poet's dwell-
ing in classical style.[21]

The move back to Mårbacka also stimulated Lagerlöf's writing.
As the new Mårbacka took shape, memories of people who had
inhabited the old estate became vivid, inspiring such works as *Liljecronas hem* (*Liliecrona's Home*, 1911)—in which the author relates,
in disguised form, the story of her grandmother—and several chapters of the memoirs that were to become the basis for the Mårbacka
books. Another work set in the region of her childhood home is
Kejsarn av Portugallien (*The Emperor of Portugallia*), which came out
in 1914. Despite the fact that this novel is a chronicle of Värmland,
the reader can sense the ominous rumblings of the Great War that
broke out in August of the same year.

Personal and Literary Relationships

Although Lagerlöf enjoyed many intellectual relationships with prominent men, like many cultivated women of her day she lived mostly in a distinctly feminine world. During her entire life, she had steadfast women friends, among them the person who meant most to her, Sophie Elkan, a woman of effervescent temperament, beautiful, witty, and well-read. She too was a writer, known for a series of historical novels. The two women were traveling companions on long trips abroad, including an extensive trip to the Near East in 1899 and 1900, when they visited the American colony in Jerusalem with the Dalecarlian farmers who had emigrated. They were frequent guests in each other's homes, discussed their books, read aloud, and criticized—often severely—contemporary literature. Sophie Elkan's charming, though somewhat neurotic, personality is reflected in several of Lagerlöf's women characters from the turn of the century; for example, Micaela in *The Miracles of Antichrist* and Gertrude in *Jerusalem*.[22]

With the move to Dalecarlia in 1897, Lagerlöf acquired another friend who came to mean much to her—Valborg Olander, a calm and methodical teacher of Swedish. She became a supporting friend in practical matters, especially when it came to copying manuscripts. Her interesting notes about the personal side of Lagerlöf are preserved in the Mårbacka archives, now in the Royal Library in Stockholm. She emphasizes the humor, spiritual strength, and superior intelligence of her famous friend. Both Valborg and Sophie were important and assertive women. They were more conventional in their tastes than Lagerlöf, and their influence on her writing was not always fortunate. A number of complications in the form of jealousy and vying for the affections of their brilliant friend were inevitable. When Sophie died, Lagerlöf had a room at Mårbacka furnished as a memorial to her friend, fellow-author, and traveling companion. To this day that room remains undisturbed.

Emotions ran high in women's circles at the turn of the century. Even if Lagerlöf appears never to have experienced a love relationship with a man, she experienced emotions usually associated with love between the sexes in her friendships with women—she knew dependence, jealousy, and the joy of warm and loving friendship. When she was in her seventies, she developed a close friendship with the Baroness Henriette Coyet, a worldly woman and the lady of a manor in Skania (Skåne), the southernmost province of Sweden. This friendship rejuvenated Lagerlöf, and for a time it fueled her creative powers. A more complex relationship developed between Lagerlöf and Ida Bäckmann, a writer known for her friendship with the poet Gustaf Fröding, whom Lagerlöf also held in high esteem. In 1944 Ida Bäckmann published the correspondence between Lagerlöf and herself.

The Public Person

Lagerlöf enjoyed all the fame possible for a writer. The zenith was, of course, the Nobel Prize. Wearing a long, gray silk gown, she graciously received the award from the king. But the fame and the money that came along with the prize brought about a multitude of problems. Appeals for help and support came from both relatives and strangers; innumerable letters poured in from people begging for money—and Lagerlöf found it difficult to refuse them. She was, behind the screen, a great philanthropist.

For Lagerlöf, as for so many others, the First World War was a period of trials, despite her residing in neutral Sweden. With her public demanding that she should devote her writing to questions of war and peace, she fell into a productivity crisis. After much anguish, she published *The Outcast* (*Bannlyst,* 1918), generally regarded as a weak novel. She was happy, however, that she finally had overcome the crisis.

The 1920s were highly productive years for Lagerlöf. She published *Mårbacka*—her first book of memoirs—and began work on the series of novels about the family called Löwensköld, a project never to be completed. A number of new features can be distinguished in the works of this period. One finds, for example, additional touches of humor and a more intimate style. Paradoxically, her general outlook on life becomes somewhat gloomy, as evidenced in her last novel, *Anna Svärd,* which reveals that Lagerlöf's earlier conception of mankind has been stripped of some of its illusions.

With the advent of Nazism in Germany in the early 1930s, Lagerlöf's relationship to her large and devoted reading public in that country became precarious, for she refused to allow either herself or her work to be exploited by Nazi propagandists. She contributed much to the efforts to help Jewish refugees and she was punished for it. As she wrote in a letter in 1933, "under the new regime,

Germany has become revengeful. They will not forgive me for helping the Jews."[23] In the same year, when a fund for intellectuals in
exile was established in Sweden, she contributed the royalties from
the Biblical legend "The Writing on the Earthen Floor" ("Skriften
på jordgolvet").

As late as the end of the 1930s, despite her failing health, Lagerlöf
confided to Ida Bäckmann that nothing was so "enchanting, captivating, almost overpowering" as to write.[24] Her last project was
a biography of her fascinating friend Sophie Elkan, a woman of
Jewish heritage. By 1940 she managed to finish two chapters about
Sophie's childhood, in which she discusses the problems of a Jewish
girl growing up in essentially non-Jewish surroundings. They were
published posthumously in the collection *From Different Times (Från
skilda tider)*.

Lagerlöf died at Mårbacka on 16 March 1940, when Hitler's
legions were beginning to hold the world in fearful suspense. As
her biographer Elin Wägner points out, while Lagerlöf's works
enjoyed the usual wave of interest given to writers for a certain time
after their death, the essence of her art is timeless. She was able to
articulate the important questions of life by going back to the
primary concerns of the people. These concerns are always topical.

Chapter Two
Gösta Berling's Saga

Gösta Berling's Saga is sometimes regarded as the most significant novel in Swedish literature.[1] When it was published in 1891, it was so new and revolutionary that it confused the critics, who found it impossible to categorize. *Gösta Berling's Saga* is, in many respects, a protest against the objective naturalism prevalent in Swedish literature of the 1880s, disregarding its tenets and reintroducing myth and fantasy into literature. It is now described in literary history as a genuine and eloquent example of the poetic renaissance movement that came to dominate Swedish literature in the 1890s.

Epic Form

Ten years passed from the day Lagerlöf received the idea for her novel until the time it was published. A series of letters from Lagerlöf to various friends, especially the well-known feminist Sophie Adlersparre, provides an insight into the development of the novel. The work is designed as a series of chapters, each of which can be read as a story complete in itself; at the same time, the book as a whole contains a unified, dramatic plot. To her own surprise and delight, Lagerlöf gradually discovered that her ability to compose was just as powerful as her creative imagination.[2] These two talents never failed her throughout her career as a writer.

Gösta Berling's Saga became a dynamic work, teeming with life and action, change and metamorphosis. Story line, psychology, style—everything is expressed in crescendos, superlatives, and paradoxes. At the same time, the novel is held together by a sober and economic artistic intent. The entire work is shaped into clear, concrete scenes, characterized by a sharp concept of reality and insightful psychological observation.

Having grown up with the literature of the 1880s, Lagerlöf not only was interested in both Zola and Strindberg, but also had assimilated their realistic code. The realistic and sociocritical elements of *Gösta Berling's Saga* have been stressed by scholars who have become increasingly interested in the question of reality, as it can be applied to Lagerlöf's entire literary production. The interplay between the real and the romantic has been called the driving force of her fiction.[3]

Lagerlöf had, however, a long-held aversion to writing about mundane everyday occurrences.[4] She was fascinated by profound and cataclysmic emotional experiences and important existential choices. In the midst of a period when Swedish prose writers were concentrating on the contemporary scene, she turned her attention toward the past and began to write about colorful characters with emotional and dramatic lives.

But it is still difficult to define what kind of a work *Gösta Berling's Saga* really is. Perhaps it is even impossible to label it as belonging to any distinct genre. While it fits into the tradition of the nineteenth-century novel, it is also closely related to the epic and cyclic form of the romance.[5] An American scholar, Elsa Olson-Buckner, has pointed out the multiplicity of epic elements in the book and shown that there is much to be said for observing it both as an epic and as a heroic saga in the traditional sense.[6] This view is supported by Lagerlöf's own description of her work in a letter to Sophie Adlersparre (15 March 1891): "It is a novel of an entire region, and it will be a colossal epic, if the spirit stands by me."

The narrative technique and the organization of the plot are typical of the epic—that is, the novel contains the episodic digressions and underlying unified plot characteristic of that genre. *Gösta Berling's Saga* consists of twenty-three chapters of varying content, which makes the book seem confusing at times and difficult for the reader to follow. But the work adheres to the traditional view that a novel should reflect life on different levels and with a great many variations. Comic and tragic events are intertwined; episodes dealing with everyday life alternate with romantic episodes to present a vision of the variety and fullness of life.

But the fragmented narrative does contain unifying elements—setting, time, and a cast of characters who reappear throughout the book. It has at its center both masculine and feminine protagonists, Gösta Berling and Major Samzelius's wife, the mistress of Ekeby. The time covered in the narrative—with the exception of the introductory chapters—is limited to one year, which extends from one Christmas Eve to the next. While the story is set in "an entire region," as Lagerlöf put it, the action is concentrated mainly in the

area around a large lake, Löven, in the province of Värmland. The
stories of the characters are closely interrelated and form more or
less clear lines and patterns throughout the novel. Thus the reader
can follow the hero, Gösta Berling, from the first chapter to the
last, even though, in true epic fashion, he is sometimes out of the
picture. One can perhaps agree with Alrik Gustafson's view that
"the real hero of *Gösta Berling's Saga* is not Gösta Berling, but the
collective character of Värmland."[7]

Elsa Olson-Buckner stresses the importance of the novel's setting
and its collective dimension. The work possesses "a choric quality,"
she writes; it depicts the soul of a society.[8] *Gösta Berling's Saga* can
be described as "a space novel," which, like the novels of Thomas
Hardy, encompasses an entire province—its nature, people, customs, and county courts. Often, all of Värmland is brought into
the perspective of the narration, a comprehensive technique that
also marks Lagerlöf's later novels. She prefers to work with large
surfaces and many characters in her field of vision and with systems
in which the balance between the social order and nature is sensitive
and easily upset. Everything is portrayed as living, animated, and
interrelated, a perspective that provides the basis for dynamic action
with moral overtones. Since the actions of individuals affect the
entire community, implicit in them is an infinite responsibility.

In *Gösta Berling's Saga,* the whole region is involved in a great,
morally determined upheaval; it assumes the character of an epic,
defined by Ezra Pound as "a poem including history."[9] Since
the book deals essentially with imagined events, it would scarcely
be rewarding to search for the reality behind the action. *Gösta
Berling's Saga* is one great fabrication. But essential for Lagerlöf's
literary method is the combination of realism and fantasy.

Reality and Myth

The realism in *Gösta Berling's Saga* manifests itself in many ways.
Although the place names are fictive, the actual setting of the story
can be found on a map of Värmland, and the industry and economic
conditions of the area form the basis of the story. The action is set
at the end of the 1820s—the end of the romantic period. Lagerlöf
evokes with much precision the atmosphere of the time—the heyday
of the great iron foundries in Värmland, the golden age of rich
foundry owners and beautiful country estates. Like many of Lagerlöf's

books, *Gösta Berling's Saga* gives evidence of her deep interest in history and her command of a whole spectrum of styles from different periods. What she sought in the past was primarily "the inner history of the people." Folkloristic material from Värmland and other regions determined the substance of *Gösta Berling's Saga,* one of the original aims of which was a cultural-historical one; Lagerlöf wanted to preserve the knowledge of customs and folklore, which she believed to be threatened.[10]

The narrative also makes use of the great treasure of fairy tale motifs and archetypes. The novel is grounded in the social history of Värmland, but it also has a symbolic dimension. As in the works of many other writers of world literature—Gogol and Gabriel García Márquez, for example—the dual levels of myth and reality form a rich artistic pattern.

Seen from the mythical perspective, the region around Lake Löven appears as an autonomous kingdom where nature is more beautiful and the people finer than elsewhere. Everything is simultaneously magnified and condensed into a unique symbolic world. The illusion of these unusual dimensions is created to a high degree by the subjectivity and enthusiastic attitude of the narrator. The first-person narrator is not merely a sober chronicler who creates the illusion of an objectively studied reality but also a passionately involved person who addresses both the readers and the characters of the story with such outcries as "O, women of bygone days!" Through this perspective of epic distance, the past acquires its significance. From a position in the empty and skeptical present, the first-person narrator describes the past with superlatives, interjections, and hyperboles. In a manner typical of the epic, the past is thus given importance and emphasis. It has something to say to "children of a later time" because "the people of olden days" were bolder and greater than those living today in matters concerning both good and evil.

Everything can be transfigured in the realm of the imagination. In this world, Löven is no ordinary lake, but "the lake of my dreams, around which I have seen gods wander." The year depicted in the novel is an exceptional period in which special powers are released; the so-called cavaliers come to power at Ekeby, and a violent storm, the "storm of God," sweeps over the land. The symbolic meaning is clear: interpreted in psychological terms, the storm represents all the powers of the soul let loose in an interplay in

which both the reader and the characters in the novel are forced to
re-examine their lives.

Plot: The Revolt of the Cavaliers

Gösta Berling's Saga is built on a bold and imaginative idea: a
group of adventurers and gallants known as the twelve cavaliers are
granted control for one year of an estate and several foundries in the
region around Lake Löven. They form a close-knit fraternity, living
for happiness and amusement, for dancing, singing, and adventure.
Everything connected with the desires and fancies of the moment
is included in their plan for a life of pleasure—a plan that, during
the course of the year, is elevated to an actual mission for the
cavaliers, for they believe that without them, the entire countryside
would be populated only by dull, plodding iron and foundry owners.

The concept of a special world wherein happiness and amusement
reign can be traced back to ancient myths, as well as to legends of
more recent times—the medieval fantasies about the Venusberg,
the legendary kingdom of *Schlaraffenland,* and, in Swedish literature,
the utopia of Per Daniel Amadeus Atterbom's *Lycksalighetens ö (The
Isle of Bliss),* where happiness and sensual pleasures are boundless.

For the most part, the utopian myth contains the notion that the
pleasures of life are threatened. Those who inhabit such a utopia
live in blissful joy until they realize that their lives of pleasure are
in reality a kind of captivity. From then on, they do all they can
to escape. This theme is present in *Gösta Berling's Saga.* Like Odysseus and his men, who for a time enjoy the voluptuous life on Circe's
island, the cavaliers too are the captives of a powerful woman. They
are given board and lodging in the "Cavaliers' Wing" of Ekeby
Manor, a magnificent estate belonging to Margarita Samzelius, the
Major's Wife and the most powerful woman in Värmland. For a
long time, the cavaliers have regarded her as their benefactress, their
kind lady whose good meals and strong drink they enjoy. But when
the truth is revealed to them that they are actually in her power,
they see her as a witch who is robbing them of their very souls,
and they swear to take revenge.

The revolt of the cavaliers against the Major's Wife is presented
in the chapters "Christmas Eve" and "The Christmas Dinner." These
two chapters, which illustrate Lagerlöf's ability to combine an in-
ventive imagination with social and psychological insight, provide

the background for the rest of the story. Although not the introductory chapter of *Gösta Berling's Saga,* "Christmas Eve" is the first
chapter Lagerlöf wrote, and it became the core and the starting point
of the entire novel. It is no coincidence that the story begins at a
time such as Christmas Eve; a number of Lagerlöf's works show how
fascinated she was with the magic of Christmas.

The Christmas Eve that introduces the joys of the cavaliers' year
of power at Ekeby has a distinct anti-Christian character. The cavaliers are enjoying more of a Dionysian celebration in the forge at
Ekeby, an appropriately dark locality, while the other people in the
region light their candles and prepare in various ways for the traditional early morning Christmas service. When Gösta Berling, the
defrocked clergyman and leader of the cavaliers, preaches to his
companions, he speaks not of the joyous message of Christmas, but
of the hedonistic pleasures the cavaliers represent and of their mission
as apostles of frivolity in a well-ordered bourgeois world.

The main figure at the celebration is, consequently, not the Christ
child but a representative of the devil, a man called Sintram, the
villain of the novel, "whose greatest pleasure was to masquerade as
the Evil One in horns and tail and hoofs and hairy hide" and who
plays an important role as the devil's messenger. On Christmas Eve,
he comes down through the chimney of the forge, complete with
cloven hooves and horns. It is he who reveals to the cavaliers that
they are living their lives of pleasure on the edge of hell, for the
Major's Wife, their benefactress, is in reality a sorceress who, through
Sintram, has made a pact with the devil. In order that she may
retain her wealth, every year she must send the soul of one cavalier
to hell. This is the mythical explanation for the fact that the cavaliers
are being consumed by their unrestrained hedonistic lives.

Sintram becomes the instrument for the cavaliers' revenge. With
Gösta Berling leading them, they draw up a contract with the Evil
One that grants them control over the seven foundries of the Major's
Wife. As in Goethe's *Faust,* the contract is written with blood from
the hero's finger, and in the manner of the folktale it is not without
an express stipulation: the cavaliers promise that, during the course
of the year, they will remain cavaliers and not do anything "sensible
or useful or effeminate." If they break their vow, they will come
under the power of the Evil One at the end of the year.

"Christmas Eve" closes with a wild dance—a ritual to seal the
pact. After the cavaliers form a ring around the leaping Sintram,

who throws himself down and drinks punch from the steaming
kettle, they too throw themselves down, forming a ring around the
kettle, which they pass from mouth to mouth. The scene becomes
an antithesis to the Christian sacrament of the Eucharist. The final
words of the chapter seem to suggest that the cavaliers will indeed,
with the help of the Evil One, become kings for a year: "his (Sintram's) golden promises still seemed to float like shining crowns
over their heads."

The dramatic scene in which the cavaliers give vent to their desire
for revenge occurs in the following chapter, "The Christmas Dinner," in which the revolution becomes a reality. Their hatred for
the Major's Wife is awakened by a concrete situation in which they
feel themselves declassed. At the sumptuous Christmas dinner at
Ekeby, they have been placed not at the main table with the Major's
Wife and her fifty guests, but at a separate table in a corner. Their
anger over being pushed aside results in an uproar of a most primitive
sort. One of them—the strong but stupid Kristian Bergh—imag-
ines that the cavaliers are being served roast crow, instead of the
more delicate roast grouse being given to all the other guests. Beside
himself with rage, he flings the grouse against the wall and breaks
out in accusations against the Major's Wife. In front of everybody,
he cries out her secret: her wealth is a gift from a former lover, and
her social position is, therefore, the result of an adulterous affair.
Since her role as a pillar of society is ill-gotten, she has no right to
insult the cavaliers.

As in a Greek tragedy, this unmasking leads to an upheaval in
the lives of the characters. The Major's Wife is driven from Ekeby,
turned out by her husband to beg on the wayside. In order to assure
the greatest possible destruction to his wife's seven foundries, the
Major gives them over to the cavaliers, who he is certain will neglect
and mismanage them. This is the psychological motivation behind
the subsequent action of the novel. At the same time, everything
has gone according to plan on the mythical level. The cavaliers have
robbed the "witch" of her riches and become masters of the district;
the power and the glory of all the world is theirs. They repeat their
pledge that they are "determined to do nothing sensible or practical
or uncavalier-like" during their year of power.

The Kingdom of Happiness—a Utopia

The great upheaval that results when the Major's Wife is driven
out and the cavaliers take over provides the background for that

which follows. While the subsequent chapters depict what seems to be a disconnected series of events, all that occurs fits into the framework of the year of the cavaliers and the conditions brought about by their reign. During this period, the brotherhood of cavaliers lives according to its hedonistic philosophy, playfully, but also with uninhibited aggression, adding zest and color to the lives of all who live around Lake Löven. The pattern reflects the king-for-a-day notion, illustrated by many most strikingly dramatic situations. For a limited period, these men, formerly considered unimportant wards of the Major's Wife, enjoy the triumph of their newly acquired splendor and power. That is how matters stand with the "poor cavaliers," as they are sometimes called.

The innovation in Lagerlöf's treatment of the utopia motif is that she introduces her utopia into a realistic society—a bourgeois order that the cavaliers promise to do their best to destroy. This leads to a series of antitheses; the Major's Wife represents the "work that brings riches" to the people, the cavaliers, "butterfly-winged joy." There is also a polarization between the masculine and the feminine; maternal and order-preserving restraints are opposed by a self-indulgent and destructive masculine attitude. *Gösta Berling's Saga* concerns itself throughout with forces and opposing forces, theses and antitheses. Even in the concluding chapter, when the Major's Wife demands of the cavaliers that they assume an important role in society, they guarantee that they will do so, but they will also work to keep happiness alive in "the ironland in iron times." All this combines to make *Gösta Berling's Saga,* with its utopian idea, an exceptionally forceful novel.

The cavaliers' platform for happiness is depicted in many different ways. On the comic level, their view of life is presented as a cheerful negation of all sober limitations. The cavaliers are no "close-fisted moneybags," no "sleepy masters on their own estates." They are free men, without home or footing, "wayfaring men, cheerful men, knights of a hundred adventures."

Although the reign of the cavaliers has aspects relating it to the aesthetic, it also contains pleasures that accentuate an essentially unaesthetic and primitively masculine side of life. Thus, whereas all the cavaliers can play at least one musical instrument, with the lot of them forming an ensemble and playing works from the classical repertoire, they also enjoy hunting and drinking bouts, and they are full of jokes and stories. Excesses of the table contribute to the picture, with feasting, bitter ale, and sweet gin representing the

Dionysian side of existence. Their pleasures are intensive and short-lived and revolve around "roses, card games, dance, and song." The rotund Squire Julius pays tribute to this blissful life in the following dithyrambic manner:

Oh, the glorious feasts! Oh, the fair shores, the proud falls! Oh, the wild adventures, the white, smooth floors, oh, life of happiness and pleasure!

But there is more to the spirit of the cavaliers than hedonism; it actually covers a broad spectrum of attitudes toward life, with great emphasis placed on freedom. The cavaliers revolt against various forms of cold formality, rigidity, and death, as well as against the order necessary to keep the society running smoothly. *Gösta Berling's Saga* deals ultimately with confrontations between life and death on many different levels and in a series of variations.

This theme provides the book with both a good deal of lively variation and a basic unity. From the standpoint of plot, the different chapters appear anecdotal and separate. But they have in common a structure in which vital feelings—represented collectively by the cavaliers—break through barriers of various kinds.[11]

Several of the episodes in *Gösta Berling's Saga* illustrate how the cavaliers stand on the side of unbridled vitality against all that is stifling and inhibiting. They uncover much that is narrow-minded, base, and rotten in their society, beginning by stripping the mask from the Major's Wife and exposing her hubris and her double standard of morality. They represent genuine, expansive love and tolerance in a stupid and self-centered existence. Chapters such as "The Churchyard" and "Plaster Saints" place the generous and loving spirit of the cavaliers in contrast to the intolerance and anticultural attitude of the established representatives of the society. In these instances, happiness becomes identical with moral courage, the ability to assert values other than material ones. The aesthetic life is also accentuated as a value, especially in its relationship to sorrow and depression. Even self-deception can be positive and necessary in a tragic situation. This wisdom can be drawn from the chapter "The Lady Musica," in which the cavaliers use their music to console a brother who has given himself over to sorrow. How the strongest power in the world, the absolute ruler Eros, conquers even the most fanatic rationalism is seen in the chapter "Amor Vincit Omnia," in which the learned Uncle Eberhard offers his great life's work—a treatise that reveals the truth of human existence—on the altar of love. Thus the various chapters about the cavaliers themselves appear as a series of examples illustrating the spectrum of happiness, as well as its power and possibilities in an existence of suffering and care.

More ambiguous are the stories that show the cavaliers' lives as bittersweet captivity, heavy with guilt. Variety and a heightened existence, such as the one that Ekeby offers, is necessary for the soul, but this knowledge exacts its price. A chapter such as "Liljecrona's Home" juxtaposes sharply the need of a great artist for an inspiring life in the whirl of events with the little life, the simple life that offers peace, quiet, and the happiness of one's own home. The chapter "Squire Julius" depicts with playful irony the unsuccessful attempt of one of the cavaliers to leave Ekeby. He proves that it is impossible to resist the attraction of the cavaliers' wing of Ekeby manor.

There are also dangerous powers inherent in the hedonism of the cavaliers, who are governed by the evil Sintram and are often described as being synonymous with nature at its wildest, casting aside barriers and established values. The spring flood that comes crashing through the dam in the chapter "The Paths of Life" symbolizes the reckless way of life characteristic of the cavaliers' year of power. "The wild chase of adventure" is a phrase that stands for the dangerous passions released during the reign of the cavaliers. These hedonistic adventurers ultimately become a marked threat to the economy and social order of the land. Family life falls into disorder in formerly peaceful homes. Iron foundries are mismanaged and the cultivation of crops left undone. At the close of the novel, the entire district has sunk into poverty and misfortune, drunkenness, and indifference—all a consequence of the cavaliers' spirit and all extremely demoralizing for the people. The chapter "Kevenhüller" depicts one of the cavaliers, out of his senses, setting fire to Ekeby. The time for self-destruction has arrived.

The burning of Ekeby provides the occasion for the brotherhood of cavaliers to be dissolved. When the year is up, they leave their paradise of happiness for the loneliness and cutting winds of reality. The dream of a utopia has ended. They are judged severely for their wastefulness and carelessness, but they are, nevertheless, not condemned. They rationalize that they have, in spite of everything, won their bet with Sintram. While it is true that they are reconciled with the Major's Wife and that they see to it that the work at the foundries begins again, these gestures are interpreted as heroic ones, fully in keeping with their proud pledge—that they would not do anything unbecoming a cavalier. The primitive and comic level on which the band of "heroes" plays out its role is carried through to the end, when the cavaliers leave the scene.

The Games that People Play around Lake Löven

As in all epics, the cast of characters in *Gösta Berling's Saga* is extensive. Contrasting sharply with the twelve-man company of cavaliers is a large number of characters, each of whom represents in his own way the life and activity of the district. Almost every chapter introduces a new character. Some appear briefly and are soon out of the story; others stand out in bold relief. Even in this her first novel, the distinctive features of Lagerlöf's manner of depicting characters can be seen. In keeping with the author's striving for objectivity, each figure is drawn with the utmost care. Even the many secondary characters (who actually can be considered only background characters) are not merely outlined, but depicted with precision and careful attention to detail—sometimes they even appear as the most three-dimensional characters in the novel.

Often, the characters are likely to take on a typological nature, becoming representatives of different qualities, and together they cover a broad scale of human attitudes. The more central the characters are, the more they represent the basic stance of the work. Gösta Berling generally supports the attitude represented by the cavalier spirit; he therefore functions more as a principle than as an individual. This trait is strengthened by the fact that he is akin to literary prototypes, such as Don Juan and Faust, and as such is a figure well-suited for the romantic period that he both lives in and embodies.

There are other figures in *Gösta Berling's Saga* reminiscent of several of the stock characters found in world literature, especially in the domain of comedy—the pedant (Henrik Dohna), the old coquette (Märta Dohna), the miser (the Broby clergyman), the old maid with fantasies of love (Mamselle Marie), and several others, including a latter-day Falstaff (Squire Julius)—characters who give evidence of Lagerlöf's extensive reading and rich knowledge of opera and theater. At the same time, however, her characters are firmly rooted in the folk tradition of Värmland. Sintram, for example, may resemble Mephistopheles in *Faust,* but he is also a devil who clearly stems from popular tales of Värmland, as well as from Nordic legends.

Mythification is an important element of Lagerlöf's character delineation. Certain figures alternate between mythical and realistic roles, sometimes in a mystifying way. Sintram, for example, may be decked out to appear as the devil of popular tales, complete with goat's horns. On one occasion, however, he appears as the Prince of Darkness himself, a frightening figure whose desire it is to destroy the entire district. At other times, he is a vision, a hallucination brought forth by human fear. His function is to personify evil, for it is he who instills evil impulses in people. Behind these images stands a realistic character, an unusually wicked foundry owner who engages in illegal affairs. In the realistic context, his plans to destroy the region are explained very simply by the fact that he has gone mad.

This double perspective occurs also in connection with the common people of the district. In the mythical sense, they appear as creatures of nature, gnomes and spirits called to life to defend the environment when it is threatened by destructive forces. At other times, they are described realistically from a sociological perspective as poor and exploited people.

This blend of myth and reality creates a lively cast of characters. In the magical light of "Christmas Eve," the cavaliers are presented as the eternal group of twelve men from legends of yore. These heroes of happiness are ironically called the Knights of the Round Table and the paladins of Charlemagne reincarnated. The forge is "an Olympus, and the cavaliers' wing a Valhalla." On the realistic level, however, the cavaliers are a group of former officers and other socially declassed men who live like parasites off those who work. In the Mårbacka series and in several short stories, these social outcasts, who in their day had belonged to the upper classes, are shown in a realistic light. That they essentially are pitiable figures, barely accepted by society, comes through at times in *Gösta Berling's Saga,* especially in the chapters in which the lives of the individual cavaliers are treated. But even if one suspects the ruins behind the

heroic facade, each cavalier is indeed a bearer of the proud message
of the joy of life.

There are also exclusively mythical figures who appear in *Gösta
Berling's Saga,* such as the Dovre witch and the Wood Nymph, who
appear among the people in a perfectly natural manner. Occasionally,
the clash between reality and myth gives rise to some rather shocking
situations, such as when the Wood Nymph walks through the
marketplace in Karlstad, the capital of Värmland, frightening both
man and beast. Both the forces of nature and human emotions are
personified, some more obviously than others. "Those icy eyes" are
a pregnant symbol for the coldness and lack of emotion of the
beautiful Marienne Sinclaire. We also meet Death, the Deliverer;
Eros, the all-conquering; fear, the witch; and spring, with its retinue
of allegorical characters. On the whole, Lagerlöf succeeds in making
her personifications believable. She possesses the myth-creating power
to get to the essence of reality.

Mythification in *Gösta Berling's Saga* is also a function of the first-
person narrator's historical distance. The people of "olden days"
stand out as being more captivating and filled with vitality than
the anemic "children of a later day." With a touch of parody, their
qualities are often heightened by superlatives. The Major's Wife is
likened to God the Father himself, and the young women of the
district are unmatched for their beauty and goodness. The cavaliers
are presented as "men whose renown will live long," masters in all
that concerns cardplaying, drinking, love, and adventure. That their
fame is founded on such exploits makes these "heroes" comic.

As a result of the exaggeration and cultivation of their eccen-
tricities, the figures are often contrasted with one another. The old
set the stage for the young; the good contrast with the evil. Individual characters also possess contrasting qualities within themselves; for example, Gösta Berling is "the strongest and the weakest"
among men. Typically, Lagerlöf—in this early work as in later
ones—carries on a kind of game with human fortunes. She does
not depict slow, continuous processes but quick, dramatic transformations. She concentrates her attention—indeed, all her knowledge of human nature—into scenes depicting the critical moments
when these sudden changes take place. Examples of such changes
can be seen in Gösta Berling himself; he appears first as a clergyman,
then as a beggar without home and hearth, before he meets the
Major's Wife, who makes him a cavalier at Ekeby. In the final

chapter, he visualizes still another calling for himself—he wants to become a village fiddler and plant a few apple trees, to be a modest tenant farmer on the shores of Lake Löven. The lives of the women are also marked by tempestuous change. They must be viewed in connection with these sudden changes of fortune, through which the characters approach a higher awareness of their social and moral destiny.

A feature typical of Lagerlöf's character depiction seen in *Gösta Berling's Saga,* as in all her works, is that the characters are clearly anchored in a specific social reality. They are placed into a nineteenth-century hierarchical society of peasants and landowners, with clear social distinction among the latter. The crown of the manors of the landed gentry is Ekeby, the home of the Major's Wife. In a chapter such as "The Old Carriages," the reader is presented with a lavish description of the splendid interior of Ekeby and its richness in household goods, food, and drink. Directly across Lake Löven from Ekeby lies Borg, a center for both romance and social prestige, where the aristocratic Dohna family lives. It is not insignificant that precisely these members of the community, who represent the very top of the social order, are presented as the most unsympathetic characters in the novel. In Märta Dohna, the joy of life has been perverted into sadism. Her victim is her polar opposite, the young countess Elizabeth, who represents the highest stage of moral perfection, the beautiful soul.

Other important estates are Björne and Berga, the homes of two other young women who figure prominently in the novel, Marienne Sinclaire and Anna Stjärnhök. While their love stories form separate story lines, they both involve Gösta Berling and describe approximately the same curve of happiness and renunciation. Marienne Sinclaire, famed throughout Värmland for her beauty, is usually regarded as the most striking character in the novel and one who might be a camouflaged self-portrait of the author. [12] In contrast to her contemporaries, whose existence is characterized by a naive acceptance of life, Marienne is possessed by the spirit of self-analysis, which has killed the spontaneity of her emotions and rendered her indecisive. She is comparable to those "children of a later day," who do not understand how to live in the direct, straightforward manner of the old Värmlanders.

The manors are at the center of the action, with the great balls and parties at Ekeby and Borg forming a natural background for exciting love stories. Just as important, however, are the journeys to and from the different houses. *Gösta Berling's Saga* is based on movement, whether it be the fast, wild chase of an adventure-packed abduction, with pursuers at the heels, or the sorrowful wanderings of a penitent pilgrim.

Outlying foundries and estates also contribute to dramatizing various aspects of experience on both the idyllic and the mundane levels. Beyond the cultivated lands is the forest, where the poor people live who, in the end, play a decisive role when they rise in protest against the misrule of the cavaliers.

While the characters who make up the world of the novel all have their distinct social place and function, on the emotional level a rare democratic attitude prevails. The existential problems are the same for everyone. *Gösta Berling's Saga* is a novel about strong and deep feelings. Love, anger, hate, and sorrow are intensified to the extreme in an almost expressionistic manner. The anger of Kristian Bergh in "The Christmas Dinner" is so strong that it leads to the overthrow of power at Ekeby. Melchior Sinclaire, the rich foundry owner, becomes so furious over his daughter Marianne falling in love with a cavalier that he is prepared to destroy his own home. The novel consists of an uninterrupted series of dramatic actions dealing with "the sorrowful passions of a heart gone wild." At the center of these passions is romantic love, "the grand conqueror," as Marianne Sinclaire calls it. Its primary object is Gösta Berling, whose path is littered with broken hearts.

Gösta Berling—the Hero

"At last the minister stood in the pulpit." Thus reads the opening sentence of *Gösta Berling's Saga,* placing directly before the reader the title character in his role as clergyman. In the same breath, the problem of guilt is also introduced. Gösta Berling, who is about to preach a sermon, is a person over whom complaints weigh heavily; he has been drunk, careless, and neglectful of his pastoral duties. It is no poor degenerate, however, who steps before the congregation to preach his last sermon, but a brilliant speaker and a young man who "could have been cut in marble and taken for an ideal of Grecian beauty." For a while, it appears as if he will win over his congregation once again, when he dazzles them with his exceptional preaching talents. But his downfall is as unavoidable as that of the Major's

Wife, and it is brought about by the same nemesis. In both cases, it is Captain Kristian Bergh, "a giant in size and strength . . . and as stupid as a mountain gnome," who acts as the instrument of fate, for both are brought to despair and degradation by Bergh's rash actions. In the next chapter, "The Beggar," Gösta Berling steals from a child in order to get money for gin. When he awakens, after sleeping off his intoxication, he decides that nothing remains for him but suicide, and he casts himself down in a snowdrift along the highway and waits for death. It is here that the Major's Wife finds him. She convinces him that he must go on living and offers him a home in the cavaliers' wing at Ekeby. With this, his "life of idleness and pleasure" begins.

The next time we meet Gösta Berling, in the chapter "Christmas Eve," seven years have passed—the magic number—and he appears as a perfect cavalier. On different occasions, he is extolled as the epitome of joy and vitality. He can play all melodies and sing all songs; though he has written no verses, he is called a poet. He also plays the courageous and extravagant hero, "a man of many achievements." Like that of a Byronic hero, his life is a series of destructive acts; he is characterized repeatedly by the epithets "wild" and "crazy."

In his relationships with women, Gösta Berling is as courtly as a page, but he is also dangerous; he has the ability to arouse the deepest and most intense passions of the young women who fall in love with him. He is considered a threat to the solid homes in the district, and two young girls even take their lives because of him. With his horse—who significantly bears the name of Don Juan— he is a master of abduction. It is a matter of typical romantic crimes, which actually enhance the glory of the hero.

Gösta Berling's function is primarily to initiate new events in the novel. He is at one with the quick pulse of the narration, the very soul of the cavaliers' whims and adventures. But his dark past is never completely out of the picture. The reader is reminded time after time that he is not only a brilliant cavalier but also a defrocked clergyman. From the beginning, he was intended to be a man of God, a representative of the divine and the moral order. But he fell short. He is, in reality, a fallen angel, one who has been "cast out by God and man." As in Goethe's *Faust,* the forces of good and evil contend for his soul. He too has his Gretchen, who in the end brings him to his senses and to the final reconciliation. In a symbolically charged scene in the penultimate chapter, "The Forest

Hut," Elizabeth Dohna loosens the ropes with which he is tied after
running off into the forest in desperation over the accusations of the
people, once again intending to take his own life. She takes on the
function of the Major's Wife at the beginning of the novel when
she convinces him that he must go on living. But her expectations
are different; she scorns Gösta Berling's heroic actions and demands
virtues other than those dictated by the cavaliers' code: self-control
and responsibility.

Ultimately, the action is meant to bring the main character into
harmony with his surroundings in order to establish a new and
better moral order. In the end, Gösta Berling, the hero who stands
apart from society and its norms, is brought back into society, both
by his marriage to the young countess Elizabeth Dohna and by
taking upon himself the responsibility for the people. The reconciliation is confirmed in the final chapter, when the Major's Wife
blesses him with her mild, maternal hands before she dies. Although
Gösta Berling has become almost like a son to her, he cannot carry
on her work as a distinguished and wealthy foundry owner. Instead,
he chooses to lead a simple life with Elizabeth, the very embodiment
of goodness. He will balance the strict moral demands she represents
with the joy inherent in his own nature. At the core, Gösta Berling's
plan to spread culture among the peasant folk is a combination of
civic responsibility and a vitality that differs completely from the
expansive hedonism of the cavaliers. Like the hero in an eighteenth-
or nineteenth-century *Bildungsroman,* Gösta Berling can be seen as
a microcosm, who not only reflects the complex of problems of an
entire society, but also becomes, ultimately, a model for its utmost
possibilities.

The Major's Wife—"King" of the District

In the great epics, functioning side by side with the hero and his
followers is usually a king, who rules over the entire kingdom; the
heroes are his vassals. To some extent, this pattern is evident in
Gösta Berling's Saga. The "king" in this novel, however, is a woman—
the Major's Wife, mistress of Ekeby—a character of powerful, even
mythic stature as befits her position. The Major's Wife represents
the entire scale of human experience, with both the masculine and
feminine poles included in her character. In her prime, she is as
strong as a man; she smokes a pipe, swears, and likes to take part

in the roaring drinking bouts of the cavaliers. But primarily she represents humanity's feminine principle, the maternal power that cares and preserves—which, from a distorted mythical aspect, is regarded as the demonic.

The Major's Wife is the only character in the novel presented to the reader in all stages of life, from the innocence of youth through the active life of middle age to the reckoning and reconciliation of old age up to the hour of her death. She experiences life in all its profound contradictions—power and degradation, happiness and unhappiness, love and hate, innocence and guilt. With her clearly defined contours, she represents humankind in all its different phases and with all its potential.

The extent of her influence is shown when she is introduced in the second chapter, "The Beggar." It is greater than that of any of the official representatives of the society. The governor of the district, the bishop, and the foundry owners all dance to her tune. Ruling over seven flourishing foundries, she governs her Värmland empire with a firm hand. She provides work for most of its people and bears the responsibility for the economy of the whole district. In addition, she is so generous that even the useless and outcast cavaliers have a place of refuge in her kingdom.

The Major's Wife calls to mind several of the many important and powerful women in the literature of the nineteenth century, especially the great female figures in Russian literature. In the works of Chekhov, Turgenev, and Aksakov, one meets women who rule over their estates with absolute sovereignty, frequently surrounded by men scarcely capable of surviving on their own. Also related to the Major's Wife are the wife of General Mansfelt in Fredrika Bremer's novel *The Neighbors* and Mrs. Alving in Ibsen's *Ghosts*. In common with the latter two, the Major's Wife conceals a deep personal misery behind her official facade; her private life is marked by secret guilt and sorrow.

In some ways, the life story of the Major's Wife is typical for a woman of the nineteenth century. Her youth is described in romantic terms, such as those frequently found in Fredrika Bremer's characterizations of young girls. Before she was forced by her family into an undesirable marriage to Major Samzelius, she was the young Margarita Celsing, the embodiment of moral perfection, "one over whose grave angels weep." Later, when she meets the handsome and generous Altringer, she becomes his lover, and upon his death she inherits his seven foundries. Lagerlöf is always tolerant of moral lapses committed for love. The Major's Wife does not regret her adultery; to the contrary, even as an old woman, she fondly cherishes the memory of her former lover. It is not this sin that has made her spiritually dead, as she believes herself to be, but the one she committed when she rejected her mother. As in other works by Lagerlöf, the sin against the fourth commandment is accorded great significance. In the course of the adulterous affair, her mother makes a long and arduous journey in order to admonish her daughter. But the daughter refuses to recognize her as her mother. After spending a day as an unwelcome stranger in her daughter's home, the mother leaves. But before she departs, she curses her daughters with a curse that echoes the eye-for-an-eye injunction of the Old Testament:

May you be disowned, as I have been disowned, repudiated as I have been repudiated! May the highway be your home, the haystack your bed, the charcoal-kiln your stove! May shame and dishonor be your reward, and may others smite you as I smite you!

She then slaps her daughter, who returns the blow. But this is not the end of it. Both the Major's Wife and her mother are plagued by the fateful curse until, shortly before the end of the novel, they are reconciled, and the curse is lifted, allowing both of them to die in peace.

The background of the Major's Wife is revealed in the chapter "The Beggar," in which she meets Gösta Berling and prevents him from committing suicide. In a long monologue, she reveals her past to the unhappy young man. This is more than merely a narrative device for exposition; the situation shows that both of the main characters are essentially alike, even though, on the surface, there appears to be a profound chasm between the rich and powerful Major's Wife and the outcast Gösta Berling. The Major's Wife proves herself to be more than merely "a dressed-up corpse," as she describes herself to Gösta. When she struggles to prevent him from committing suicide, she is also trying ultimately to prove that she is not completely divorced from the moral life she led in her youth.

When Gösta Berling first meets the Major's Wife, she is a woman with a somewhat masculine image. She is in the midst of her practical work, "on her way home from the charcoal kilns, with sooty hands and a clay pipe in her mouth, dressed in a short, unlined sheepskin jacket and striped homespun skirt." The next time she appears, in the chapter "The Christmas Dinner," she is dressed in silk and pearls and is hostess at the festive dinner table. It is in this setting that her downfall takes place. As in the world of tragedy, it happens just when the protagonist is at the peak of her power, when she believes herself to be secure, surrounded as she is by tokens and symbols of influence and dignity. But fate—always a strong force in Lagerlöf's fictive world—brings her down.

There is also a sociological explanation for the Major's Wife losing her power to the cavaliers. Her power and elevated social position are based on her illicit relationship with Altringer and are, therefore, insecure. As a woman, she has no legal rights, and her husband can legally deprive her of her economic power, if he so desires. In depicting how the incompetent and wicked major could, without further ado, drive his wife of many years out of the house, Lagerlöf describes a situation that was legally correct in the time in which her story is set.

While the apparent reason for the downfall of the Major's Wife is her adultery, Lagerlöf seeks for deeper causes. Clearly, her weak point is the sin against her mother, which makes the upheaval not only possible, but unavoidable. Remembering her mother's curse, she casts aside her social role and embraces her private fate as a penitent. During the course of the year the cavaliers are in power, she wanders, alone and confused, along her penitent's path to her mother, now over ninety, who lives far away in the forests of the North. This mother figure is mostly a mythical symbol for the absolute moral demands that life places on the individual. The Major's Wife finds her mother in the milk house, skimming the cream from the milk in the many copper pans that stand on long shelves all around the room, a task so delicate that she would never entrust it to anyone else. When she entrusts this task to her daughter, the Major's Wife knows that she has been forgiven. (It would be hard to think of a more Freudian way to resolve the mother-daughter conflict.)

The Major's Wife stays on with her mother until the old woman dies shortly before Christmas—that is, shortly before the year of the cavaliers is up. The Major's Wife is then free to return to Ekeby. Her life, too, is completed, and death awaits her. In the last stage of her life, she returns to a state of moral innocence, once again becoming Margarita Celsing, whose face radiates her beautiful soul.

The circle is closed. She has re-established the vital and important contact with the self she lost so many years ago; the moral system of values that life once robbed her of has been restored. The mission of man to act as God's image on earth has been thwarted, but reconciliation is possible—a fundamental idea which, illustrated in almost archaic terms by the life of the Major's Wife, appears again and again in various forms throughout much of Lagerlöf's fiction.

The Collective Action of the Novel

The fate of the Major's Wife is the primary moral paradigm of the novel. The need for the truth about her life to be revealed and the sin to be atoned for is the dramatic framework on which the narrative is built. More than any other figure in the novel, the Major's Wife is also the incarnation and representative of the entire district. Whatever affects her personally affects the community as well. At the same time she pursues her own fate, she anticipates and demonstrates the personal trials all men must go through. The crises in the lives of the younger women in the novel are particularly reminiscent of those experienced by the Major's Wife. The closest parallel to the moral problems of the Major's Wife can be seen clearly in the life of the young countess, who also becomes a penitent, forced to leave her home and suffer the fate of the outcast.

Because the Major's Wife stands apart from most of the action during the year of the cavaliers—the important deeds, and misdeeds, of her life occurred in the past—she takes on an additional important function as observer and commentator. Even before the hedonistic way of life gains a foothold among the people around Lake Löven, she prophesies the day of reckoning that will come when she is no longer able to uphold the old order. As early as the fateful Christmas party, she pleads, "Who can stand when I fall?" She applies to herself the myth of the old woman who holds the winds of heaven captive, and when the cavaliers take over, there is no protection from the ravages of the storm. In terms reminiscent of the Old Testament, she prophesies that "the storm of God" will sweep over the land, striking all who live in it.

"The storm of God" becomes an affirmation of the fact that the moral order is upset. Everyone in the district is drawn into a period marked by trials and revelations. The cavaliers are the leavening agents in this process, which takes on a somewhat cosmogonical

dimension.[13] All of nature—men, animals, inanimate objects—are
swept up in "the wild chase of adventure," a witches' cauldron of
elemental forces. All manner of threats hang over the land and are
released in the form of natural catastrophes, primarily the prolonged
drought that leads to famine.[14] As is so often the case when the
element of fire is concerned, the burning of Ekeby in the chapter
"Kevenhüller" marks the end of a process and the beginning of
something new. The phoenix must rise from the ashes.

In the end, a counteroffensive against the "forces of devastation"
rises in the entire district. On the mythical level, the spirits of
nature rise in revolt. They protect the vegetation and produce, the
basis of life. On the social level, the revolt manifests itself in the
peasants' march upon Ekeby. Eventually, the rich join together with
the poor in order to save the district from total destruction. And
finally the cavaliers, with Gösta Berling leading them, become involved in the work of reorganizing the society.

Ultimately, the action takes the shape of a dialectical interplay,
in which good and evil vie for dominion. God and the devil are
clearly seen in the final struggle over the Lake Löven country. The
cold, calculating Sintram plans to destroy the region. But like a
Christ figure, Captain Lennart, "the pilgrim of God" who sacrifices
his life for the good of the community, saves it from the curse of
evil, becoming a model for public consciousness.

Out of the chaos arises, finally, a humane and harmonious world,
a new utopia, where peace, fellowship, and joy reign. The return
to order reaches such an extent that everyone begins to work again
with industriousness and enthusiasm. The steel hammer at Ekeby
forge, which had been idle during the year the cavaliers managed
Ekeby, is set into operation by the cavaliers on the Christmas Eve
that marks the end of the reign.

The primary result of the self-assessment that takes place at the
end of the year, however, is renewal. The fruit of the reconciliation
is a new system of values, a system in which virtue and joy are
united. This synthesis replaces the period of unrest characterized by
great opposing forces, which Gösta Berling describes as a "year of
joy and adversity and happiness and grief." When the Major's Wife
sums up the experiences of the year, she notes that the storm of
God clearly was necessary and that "all has been for the best."

In the organization of the collective plot, Lagerlöf works with
several mythical models. One suspects that behind the overall action

there is a primary group of myths from the Bible—the fall of man, paradise, and the millenium. When the Major's Wife returns home in the last chapter, she believes that she has traveled to "a holy land," where peace has gained entry. Lagerlöf refers directly to the myth of the twilight of the gods when she summarizes events as if they were mighty conflicts fought out by heroes and giants on the shores of Lake Löven. As in Old Norse legends, the battles are also followed by a harmonious golden age. "I could create myths about the sun, fire, light, groves, and rivers—with all the naiveté of primeval man," Lagerlöf wrote in a letter while she was working on *Gösta Berling's Saga*.[15] This mythical line of thought saturates the novel and welds the individual stories together into a meaningful whole, where reconciliation is of primary importance.

The theme of the great upheaval also has a background in Lagerlöf's contemporary world. Thoughts of revolution ran high during the period when she was working on *Gösta Berling's Saga*. At the close of the 1880s, there was fear of a workers' uprising, and in 1889 the hundred-year anniversary of the French Revolution was commemorated with demonstrations and "Bastille festivals" in various parts of Sweden. Within this context, Thomas Carlyle's book, *The French Revolution,* became timely for many writers; for Lagerlöf, it was profoundly important. Earlier, she had read with enthusiasm Carlyle's *On Heroes, Hero-Worship, and the Heroic in History*.[16] Now the great Scottish moral philosopher provided her with a perspective on her material and the instruments for managing it. The style of *Gösta Berling's Saga* reflects to a certain extent Carlyle's tendency for apostrophizing and subjectivity. Above all, Carlyle's work encouraged her when the collective action of her novel was taking shape. She explains the rhythm in the structure of the novel as follows: "Spring is the time of dissolution, summer is full of small idylls and apparent calm, autumn is *'la culbute générale'* and Christmas the beginning of making amends."[17] (The expression *la culbute générale* is Carlyle's term for the French Revolution.) This is the clearest contemporary evidence that Carlyle's book was indeed significant for Lagerlöf's work.[18] It is apparent that *The French Revolution* helped her to give form to her personal experiences. She too had lived through an upheaval in her own existence when she was cut off from the roots of her homeland. In a letter she wrote after the publication of *Gösta Berling's Saga,* she affirmed the fact that the idea of revolution originated in her own experience of a social transformation with moral overtones:

> And I took it upon myself to describe a little revolution, such as the kind which occasionally sweeps over even a small community, when suddenly one family after the other is broken up or cast into upsetting circumstances, and then, finally, with feelings of guilt and fear of punishment, everybody summons up his courage and tries to lead a better life. I myself once experienced something similar.[19]

Lagerlöf clearly transferred the experience of her own upheaval in Värmland in the 1870s to the romantic world she creates in her book.[20] This explains the double perspective of the action in *Gösta Berling's Saga*. The narrator observes the drama taking place around Lake Löven with a mixture of admiration and horror.

This combination of love and criticism is found in the works of many writers who depict provincial life, above all, perhaps, in those of the great Russian writers. Lagerlöf's own divided feelings about her past life provide the foundation for the basic tension of the novel. But *Gösta Berling's Saga* would not be considered an important work today if it were only a personal document or a historical chronicle. Its appeal lies in its ultimate concerns: human joy and guilt, not only in the time in which it was written, but in the present as well.

Chapter Three
From Dalecarlia to Jerusalem
Jerusalem: Reality and Fiction

Lagerlöf's third novel, the two-volume work *Jerusalem* (1901–2), can be described as a novel of rustic life, a tale of emigration, and a story of love. Perhaps it is more accurate to say that it is a book about life decisions: it deals with hard moral conflicts and their solutions. In many ways, *Jerusalem* contrasts with *Gösta Berling's Saga.* Lagerlöf's first novel is a narrative that displays a kind of inherent happiness. This is evident in its manner of presentation, its rapt enthusiasm over nature, people, and life itself; it is expressed in the exuberance of the language, with its superlatives and exclamatory style, along with the involvement of an emphatic first-person narrator. With its exaggerated style, the book, in places, gives the reader a dizzying experience of the inner pulse of existence. In *Jerusalem,* by contrast, feelings are much more subdued. The spontaneity is restrained, with the narrator hidden behind an objective, Hemingwayesque manner of presentation. Parts of the novel are dominated by choppy dialogue, and the narrative technique relies on the implied rather than the explicit. The language also has far greater unity than that of *Gösta Berling's Saga.* In a manner approaching interior monologue, Lagerlöf depicts more closely the thoughts of her individual characters than she did in her earlier novel.

In organization, structure, and plot, *Jerusalem* still bears considerable similarity to *Gösta Berling's Saga,* with Lagerlöf perfecting her special method of combining an episodic structure with a many-faceted plot. Like *Gösta Berling's Saga, Jerusalem* is a monumental work of epic proportion dealing with a social upheaval that affects an entire region. Here too, changes that occur in the lives of the characters force them to examine their values and probe existential questions.

Jerusalem, however, has a much stronger basis in reality than *Gösta Berling's Saga.* The story concerns a religious revival that causes an upheaval in a peaceful, conservative rural section of Sweden—an occurrence common to many places in Scandinavia during the last years of the nineteenth century. A band of farmers from a parish in Dalecarlia (the west-central province to which Lagerlöf moved in 1897) forms a religious sect and ultimately emigrates to Jerusalem to join an American religious colony.

The first part of *Jerusalem* relates how the parish is invaded by new doctrines that create enmity among the parishioners. One of the revivalist preachers, Hellgum, is the leader of a sect that practices a kind of Christian socialism. The story culminates in the decision of his followers to emigrate and in their final departure. Lagerlöf successfully controls the main thread of her narrative, as she weaves a complex of psychological problems into her story.

In the second part, *The Holy City,* the reader meets the colonists in the Holy City. The Swedes have almost succumbed to various trials and tribulations—illness, depression, conflicts, and difficulty in adjusting to the climate. But the book ends on a harmonious note. A reconciliation of sorts takes place, along with the renewal of connections between the colonists and their homeland.

Jerusalem is based on an actual happening. Lagerlöf had read a newspaper account of a group of thirty-seven farmers from Nås, a parish in Dalecarlia, who in 1896 sold their land and emigrated to the Holy City to live in a commune and wait for the coming of Christ. They joined the American colony, which had been established earlier in Jerusalem and whose core group was made up of Americans of Swedish descent. Lagerlöf was seized by both surprise and admiration for this enterprise, the unusual and "wildly" romantic aspects of which captured her fancy. Later in life she characterized the emigration as a "noble undertaking" by the Swedes.[1]

Within a few years she gathered enough material for her novel. Accompanied by her friend Sophie Elkan, she traveled to Jerusalem and met the Swedish colonists, who believed that God had sent the two women to them. She also became acquainted with the leader of the American colony, Mrs. Spafford, known as the mother of the colonists—a woman who appears in the novel as Mrs. Gordon. Mrs. Spafford originally came from Norway but had emigrated to Chicago. She founded the colony in Jerusalem because of a mystic experience she had had after a shipwreck. She was a passenger on the steamship *Ville du Havre* when it sank in 1881, a catastrophe as widely talked about in its day as the sinking of the *Titanic* in

1912. While Mrs. Spafford's four children perished in the disaster, she herself was miraculously saved, emerging from the experience with the belief that she had been spared in order to fulfill a special purpose. Upon her return to Chicago, she established a sect based on the idea of a Christian socialist community. Together with a man named O. H. Larsson, a Swedish-American, the Hellgum of Lagerlöf's novel, she then founded the American colony in Jerusalem, which the Dalecarlian farmers joined in the summer of 1896.

Lagerlöf describes the shipwreck with a dark realism in the chapter "Loss of 'L'Univers' " in the first part of the novel.[2] Mrs. Gordon experiences her mystic revelation while floating in the water after the shipwreck, awaiting the death to which she had reconciled herself. She believes that she hears voices which "resolved themselves into clear and powerful words." The voices cry out the word *Unity* three times, which Mrs. Gordon interprets as a message from God bidding her to establish a religious community. It is this idea of unity and brotherly love that becomes the main component of the doctrine that Hellgum later preaches to the Dalecarlian farmers.

In preparing to write her story of the emigration to Jerusalem, Lagerlöf conducted her research as if she were writing a documentary novel. She meticulously recorded her observations when she visited the colony. One of her notes, for example, reads:

Mrs. Sköldberg red hair. Karolina Larsson. Jon Johnson baker. Ti Pers Lars. His daughter was the friendly one with the hat. Josef Larsson small with a goatee. Henning's Katarina weaving stockings. Israel's Brita at the loom. Josef Larsson's wife. Carded. Tilda Holmström's sewing machine.

Upon her return to Sweden, Lagerlöf visited Nås to meet relatives and acquaintances of the emigrants. She also wanted to meet those who had chosen to remain at home, in order to consider the emigration from their perspective. She brought with her presents, letters, and greetings from friends and relatives in the colony. According to a description in a letter of Sophie Elkan who accompanied Lagerlöf, the visit in Nås was a very moving one.[3]

But although Lagerlöf took extreme care to immerse herself in the concrete situation of the emigrants, and was at pains to preserve the fictionality of her story, *Jerusalem* is by no means a documentary novel. To begin with, the main characters, the Ingmarssons, have no direct counterparts among the emigrants—Lagerlöf herself has pointed out that she had chosen as her model for the Ingmarssons some of her neighbors at Mårbacka, a farm family named Olsson.[4] It is also noteworthy that she does not give a name to the place from which the emigrants set out; she simply mentions the parish in which the old Ingmarssons lived. Nor is any exact time of the emigration mentioned.

Jerusalem can scarcely be called a realistic depiction of Swedish farm life, even though the reader is allowed to participate in the everyday life of the farmers; the honest smell of the farm is simply not there. When the first part of the novel came out there was, along with the overwhelming praise, some negative criticism from radical circles, faulting Lagerlöf for idealizing the farmers. But Lagerlöf's intention was not to strive for verisimilitude in her description of life in the Swedish countryside. In a revealing letter to Bjørnstjerne Bjørnson, she discusses various methods of portraying farmers. She wanted, in her novel, to follow neither the path of stark realism nor that of exaggerated romanticism; she chose instead the stylized Nordic model that Bjørnson himself set up in his tales of country life in Norway:

But then, when I had to deal with my material, I could not have received more help from anyone than from you. We already have enough ugly and witty and realistic and overly romantic portrayals of rural life, but you are the one who has examined this life with the most love and with a feeling for its beauty. It was, therefore, with the thought of your rustic novellas that I was able to put myself in the proper mood for writing. And I want now to acknowledge this with the greatest appreciation. (12 December 1901)

That this acknowledgement is more than merely a matter of politeness can be seen in the book itself; the depiction of the people's lives and customs have certain aspects in common with Bjørnson's descriptions of country life. Furthermore, as Lagerlöf points out in her letter to Bjørnson, she was also influenced by the Icelandic sagas, and not only with regard to style. The emigration from Norway to Iceland depicted in the Icelandic family sagas served as a pattern for her when she wrote about the Swedish emigrants.[5] It is also likely that Lagerlöf found inspiration in the works of Scandinavian authors other than Bjørnson. Contemporary Danish fiction could have provided her with impressive models. Henrik Pontoppidan's

The Promised Land, for example, is an important novel that deals with a religious revival among Danish country folk.

Several letters written while she was working on *Jerusalem* reveal that Lagerlöf was consciously striving to break away from what she calls "the eloquent words," and to "write grandly and truly, and not just paint word pictures."[6] She had come to regard the style of *Gösta Berling's Saga* as showy and ornamental, in contrast to *Jerusalem*'s folkloric style.[7] But she feared at the same time that the book would lack the fullness and narrative richness of her earlier books. She was afraid that the so-called cultivated public would not want to read about farmers, that they would find them too simple and dull and their problems uninteresting.[8] But her fears were unfounded. With *Jerusalem,* she conquered the broader reading public and the elitist critics as well. People began to compare her with Homer and to mention her name in connection with the Nobel Prize for Literature.

The Ingmarssons

Like *Gösta Berling's Saga, Jerusalem* deals with a large number of characters who, in their different ways, are representative of their region. At the center of the novel is also a group of persons with a unifying aim, an identical plan for their lives. These are the Ingmarssons, a family similar to those found in the Icelandic sagas. The Ingmarssons are the most powerful people in the district. The members of the family can be regarded as a single individual, since their personal characteristics have been condensed into a type. The head of the family always bears the name Ingmar Ingmarsson, a name regarded as a guarantee of the greatest possible intelligence, honor, and ability to lead. Ingmar is described as a genuinely ugly man, with a protruding nether lip; in addition, he is so taciturn and slow that people who do not know him believe him to be rather stupid. In a way, he typifies for Lagerlöf the well-to-do-farmer. To portray a farmer as handsome was apparently unthinkable for her. In any event, Lagerlöf associated handsome men with the culture of the manor: Ingmar Ingmarsson stands in direct contrast to Gösta Berling. In the case of the Ingmarssons, the accent is on their hidden inner qualities. Once they are revealed, these qualities become important in a dramatic and creative way.

While the Ingmarssons are solid, practical folk, they are also moral supermen of sorts. They live according to the ethics of their own family—a code of honor passed down from father to son and characterized by a strong passion for justice. Their guiding principle is to not fear man, but to "walk in the ways of God," and not be satisfied with any action or situation until they are certain that it is "compatible with the will of Our Lord." These are not merely Christian slogans for the Ingmarssons; they are the expression of a deeper, universal code of ethics.

"The Peace of God"

The story of the Ingmarssons develops in three stages. The family is introduced in "The Peace of God," a Christmas story of 1898 that centers on the problem of conscience. One Christmas night, in a howling snowstorm, the old patriarch Ingmar Ingmarsson becomes lost in the forest. Unable to find his way back to the farm, he sinks defeated in the snow and fantasizes about his imminent funeral. It would be a stately affair, with many honors and distinctions bestowed upon him. The description of his vision demonstrates his elevated position in the community, and there is also a touch of hubris in his manner of anticipating the many honors that would be shown him. The reader assumes that the old farmer's presumptuousness will eventually bring down retribution. This is what indeed happens, but—as is typical for Lagerlöf—in a surprising and ironic manner.

Ingmar is miraculously saved by finding protection in the den of a bear. The bear sniffs at him and moves over to make room for him. On the next day, Ingmar is able to return safely home to the farm, where everyone has been anxiously looking for him. It is now that the fateful action begins: Ingmar goes out into the forest to shoot the bear. But the animal attacks him first, mauling him to death.

While this incident comes as a surprise, it nevertheless has been carefully presaged by omens and by fears expressed by the farmer's old wife, who sits alone at the farm while the men go hunting. Because the family is violating both the Christian demand for mercy and the Peace of God—the primitive, popular concept of the peace that exists between all creatures of nature at Christmas time—she is certain that punishment will follow. The death of her husband fulfills her most fearful suspicions.

In the short story, there is a suggestion of a boundary between the aggressive sphere belonging to men and the sphere of women—

the home and carefully upheld standards. The power of these standards can, if necessary, make possible a radical breach of time-honored customs. This happens when the family, now led by Ingmar's widow, decides not to have a stately funeral for old Ingmar. Penance demands humility.

This submission to moral and mythical demands contrasts with an equally intensive self-assurance in social and communal questions: "The sons of Ingmar fear nobody, and there is no one they need to step aside for." In Lagerlöf's earlier works, those who declare themselves independent are usually outlawed. This is not true in the case of the Ingmarssons; on the contrary, they are the leaders of the community.

The Short Story "The Sons of Ingmar"

In a subsequent, longer story, "The Sons of Ingmar," published in the yearbook *Svea* in 1900, Lagerlöf returns to the family she had introduced in "The Peace of God." The story—one of the most beautiful in the Swedish language—later became the introduction to the novel *Jerusalem*. Here too, the main concern is the question of guilt and punishment, but with a weightier moral conclusion. The story—and consequently the whole of *Jerusalem*—begins with a direct and simple introduction: "A young farmer was plowing his field one summer morning." In a flashback that takes the form of an imaginary dialogue, the young plowman explains his sensitive and tragic situation. His fiancée Brita is in prison for the murder of their child—a not uncommon crime in nineteenth-century Sweden. She committed the deed out of misery and a desire to take revenge upon Ingmar, who had not married her by the time she was ready to give birth. With the day of her release at hand, the question of what is to be done with her becomes acute. One solution is to have her emigrate to America. Ingmar's authoritarian mother and Brita's respectable father agree that that is the best way to solve the family problem, and they expect Ingmar to go along with their plan.

But he is hesitant. He finds that he cannot seek advice from those around him; he looks instead for a sign of how he should act in a greater, mythic context. When he goes out to the field and plows, his fantasy carries him up to the halls of heaven, in order that he may receive guidance from his ancestors. He seeks support in the collective moral experience of his clan. But his ancestors give him no direct indication of how he ought to act. This is an existential moral question, which the young person must always, over and over again, decide for himself. The moral system established by the family is a starting point and an aid, but it carries with it demands and responsibilities. The theme of the story is this balance between the choice of the individual and the traditional morality.

The major key that sets the tone and rings through the light, summer atmosphere of the introduction indicates that all will end well. But as always in Lagerlöf, the manner in which the problem is solved is full of surprises. In line with the story's fairy tale structure, the hero encounters both hindrances and helpers in striving to accomplish his task. He must also summon up all his courage once he has made his decision. Finally he attains his victory, again according to the fairy tale pattern, as he gains fame and honor throughout his community.

First, and most important, Ingmar must overcome the conventions that characterize his environment. His most formidable opponent is his mother, a woman related to the dictatorial women of the Icelandic sagas. As a widow, she is the family authority, whereas her son is still regarded as Little Ingmar. Her task is to re-establish the honor of the family after the shame brought upon it by Brita's infanticide. She has on her side the girl's own father, who also possesses considerable authority in his capacity as senator. Ingmar's ambition to follow his father's example and become the leader of the parish is in accord with the ideas of his more experienced elders; moreover, it is possible that Brita (who never loved him) still hates him. She was, after all, driven to her desperate deed because he had postponed their wedding for economic reasons. All these are obstacles in the young man's path, presenting him with the test that will be decisive for his life, that will give him his own identity and change him from Little Ingmar to Big Ingmar.

Behind Ingmar's calculations are feelings of guilt, as well as the insight that Brita has discovered something essentially negative about the members of his family: their stinginess and thick-headedness, and their lack of understanding for anything beyond practical concerns. He undoubtedly shares the girl's unhappiness. But most important, despite his denial of it, his love for Brita is still alive in him. It is a latent and fragile feeling, one that is relatively powerless against the attempts of those around him to prevent him from taking action. Against all odds, Ingmar finally overcomes his indecision, dresses himself in his best clothes, hitches up the horses, and goes to the jail.

The problem is not yet solved, for the young people must come to an agreement satisfactory to both of them. This coming to terms signifies a turning point in the story. Respectability and social status become unimportant in the face of the power inherent in their love and reconciliation. As is often the case in Lagerlöf, feelings overcome all barriers.

Ingmar's moral decision defies not only convention but also the wishes of his elders, making the novella, among other things, a story of the passing of generations and the conflict among them. Ingmar's mother is especially adamant. When her son comes home with Brita, she declares, "I'll not sleep one night under the same roof with the likes of her." But she gives in when the dean of the parish church appears and enthusiastically tells her that the young farmer's moral act has overcome the negative opinion of the community: "Ingmar will be a credit to us all, as his father before him was." He guarantees that in the future everyone in the parish will regard the young man as Big Ingmar, the head of the family and the proper leader of the community. The son thereby gains a victory over his mother. Now he too can adopt, as his own, the family motto "to walk in the ways of God." Once again the moral code of the Ingmarssons has proved itself superior to the standards set by the community.

Like *The Peace of God, The Sons of Ingmar* has an inherent feminist message. Brita certainly committed a horrible crime when she killed her child, but the story shows clearly how she was driven to it. Ultimately, the question concerns the rights of women and children and the role of love in relation to the obligations of the patriarchal tradition.

Lagerlöf received the idea for *The Sons of Ingmar* from a short newspaper article.[9] As she wrote to her publisher when the story was finished, the subject had "such great possibilities for expansion that it certainly could fill a novel."[10] The story in itself is unrelated to the main theme of *Jerusalem* (i.e., religious revival and emigration). It serves nonetheless as an appropriate introduction to the series of situations depicted in the novel that are brought about by religious unrest and which require decisive action. The morality of the Ingmarssons is creative; it is not enough merely to tread along on the traditional path when one walks in "the ways of God. " The attitude resulting from this creative morality has a certain affinity with the radical religiosity we meet as the story continues.[11] The Ingmarsson family has in it the stuff of nonconformists and emigrants. And the story of love and guilt—the central theme of the novel—has points in common with the drama presented in the introduction. The novel continues, with a more elaborate orchestration, to confront the problems brought about by love, ambition, and moral demands.

Religious Revival and Existential Decision

The Ingmarssons become the main characters in the book about the religious revival and the emigration. But after concentrating on the family in the introduction, Lagerlöf extends her story so that it concerns the parish as a whole. Even the religious movement is described as a dramatic power directed against the official representatives of the parish. The powerless pastor is the first to be eliminated by the new radical religiosity; he is perceptive enough to foresee the consequences of the movement, yet he is unable to do anything about it. The energetic schoolmaster builds a mission house in order to be able to control the religious ferment, but the results of his efforts are contrary to his purpose. He eventually conjures up powers that he cannot hold in check with his schoolmasterly methods, and the conservative order of the community is upset by the spirit of rebellion. Finally, when the radical sect led by Hellgum is consolidated, it appears that it will gain power over the established farm community—especially when its teachings gain ground at the Ingmar farm, the center of the parish. The farm is now run by Karin Ingmarsdotter, who took it over upon the death of her father, the Ingmar of the introductory chapter. She is described as the bearer of the typical Ingmarsson family traits and as an important representative of the family. After a series of unfortunate personal experiences, she becomes a fanatic follower of Hellgum, bringing her husband Halvor along with her. Other members of the old and powerful Ingmarsson family also join Hellgum's sect; they in fact constitute its core.

But the young hero of the book remains apart from the group. This is Ingmar, Karin's younger brother, who according to custom ought to be the owner of Ingmar Farm. But since his inheritance

had mysteriously disappeared, the young man is poor, and the
possibilities for him to walk in the footsteps of his forefathers are
negligible. He bears a secret sorrow over the fact that he will not
be able to acquire the family farm. The reader suspects, however,
that the story will follow the fairy tale pattern—a poor boy who
one day will come into fame and fortune. As in the introductory
story, the people who appear in Ingmar's life both hinder and help
him on the way to his goal.

First, a sensitive personal conflict develops between Ingmar and
Karin. For a time it appears as if Ingmar will be persuaded to join
the sectarians, but while many of the other young people in the
parish are swayed by the religious fervor, he takes an opposing stand
in the end. He chooses to follow his own conscience and the moral
code of his ancestors, which, according to custom, each new Ingmar
is duty bound to carry out. The new sect consequently causes a rift
between brother and sister.

In the center of her story of emigration, Lagerlöf thus places,
paradoxically, a person firmly rooted in his native soil and its traditions, who does not join those who want to leave it. On the other
hand, she does not cast her main character in the role of ardent
opponent of Hellgum and his followers; this would be too easy.
Instead, she gives the opposing role to several of the minor characters, primarily Strong Ingmar, a tenant farmer closely connected
to the Ingmarsson family. As for Ingmar Ingmarsson, there is much
in his character that makes him receptive to the religious movement.
There is a certain correspondence between the Ingmarsson way of
thinking and that of the sectarians; on the surface, the family's old
motto "to walk in the ways of God" appears identical with the new
way that Hellgum preaches. This similarity creates an interesting
dialectic between Ingmar's inherited moral code and Hellgum's new
Christian socialism. Ultimately, however, it becomes clear that the
Ingmarsson way of thinking differs fundamentally from Hellgum's
teachings. When Ingmar realizes this and decides not to follow the
movement, the question of power is brought to a head. The religious
fanatic Hellgum becomes Ingmar's rival for the leadership of the
parish, which historically has belonged only to a member of the old
Ingmarsson family. The religious movement has gained a firm hold
on several of the parish women. When Hellgum ingratiates himself
with Gertrude, the schoolmaster's daughter whom Ingmar loves,

the competition between Hellgum and Ingmar moves into the personal sphere as well.

The conflict between the two competitors is solved in a strange turn of events: Ingmar ends up defending Hellgum in a dramatic fight in which three enemies of Hellgum are brutally beating him. When the fight is over, Ingmar arranges for Hellgum to return to America. It appears now as if the religious upheaval will subside and that everything in the parish will return to normal. But the enthusiasm is rekindled when Hellgum writes from America, urging the members of the sect to affiliate themselves with the American colony in Jerusalem. At an ecstatic meeting at Ingmar farm, a number of sectarians receive the call to go to the Holy Land. This causes the dissolution of unity in the parish and makes inevitable a series of heartbreaking separations: a son leaves his old father, and young daughters leave their loving parents who oppose the movement. Many families break up, causing a deep rift in the community. The conflict is demonstrated again in the antagonism between Ingmar and his sister Karin in the dramatic struggle over Ingmar Farm, which builds up to one of the most tense and tragic moments of the novel.

The Drama of Ingmar Farm

Karin Ingmarsdotter, the most ardent of the pilgrims to Jerusalem, is willing to sacrifice the family farm. She intends to sell it to the highest bidder in order to get the money needed for the emigration. There is a risk that the farm will end up in the hands of strangers who care nothing for the long-standing traditions the farm represents—a threat that demonstrates clearly what a danger the religious revival is for the community. The conflict is both developed and resolved in the chapter entitled "The Auction." The action comes to a head in the manner of a classical tragedy, in which the reader can follow, step by step, the dealings connected with the sale of the farm while all the tradition-laden farm implements and household articles are auctioned off. Like a solitary tragic figure, Ingmar is witness to the drama; he appears to be drowsy and indifferent, but actually he is struggling with the most difficult decision of his life. Will he choose the possibility that has been presented to him for gaining possession of his beloved ancestral farm? He can do this if he marries Barbro, a girl whose rich father had promised

her Ingmar Farm as a wedding gift. But then he must give up
Gertrude, the young woman he loves. In the end, he chooses the
farm over his love.

Ingmar's decision is a turning point in the story. It is a sign that
something has been stabilized in the parish. When he takes over
the family farm, he creates a counterbalance to the dynamics of the
religious movement. In the long run, his decision is a positive one,
for it guarantees that the established values of the rural community
will be upheld.

But on the personal level, Ingmar's action is a betrayal, a tragic
decision that determines the course of all future events. In a following chapter, entitled "Gertrude," Ingmar's young, forsaken fiancée is described, with all her despair and desire for revenge. Her
sorrow threatens to slip over into madness, but she is saved by a
visionary religious experience and decides to join the pilgrims to
Jerusalem.

In the gripping conclusion of the first part of *Jerusalem*, Lagerlöf
depicts the long procession of the emigrants to the train station and
their irrevocable separation from their birthplace, its nature, and
its people. In the second part, we meet the emigrants in the Holy
Land.

The Problem of Guilt

The second part of the novel appears at first to be an independent
story of the suffering of the Swedes in the Holy City. In a series of
episodes, the hardships of the colonists are described with a realism
stronger than is found earlier in Lagerlöf's writings. Karin Ingmarsdotter's husband Halvor dies of a heart attack when he discovers
that the Swedish cemetery has been desecrated, a young girl is killed
by sunstroke, and Gertrude is once again slipping into the darkness
of mental derangement.

In a situation in which the colony appears to be on the verge of
ruin, a major reversal takes place in the dramatic and effective
manner typical of Lagerlöf. Ingmar Ingmarsson appears suddenly in
the colony and joins his countrymen. He has come to the Holy City
as a humble penitent with one single purpose: to atone for his wrongs
against Gertrude. His mission is to take her home from Jerusalem,
just as his father once led his fiancée home after her imprisonment.

In the emigration novel, however, the basic problem of the introductory story is considerably more varied and dramatic.

Ingmar's guilt forms a bridge that spans the parish and the colony.
As soon as he reaches his destination, the point of view is largely
transferred from the colonists to him. This effective shift enables
the reader to watch as Ingmar's wait-and-see attitude toward the
colonists changes into one of great respect. Little by little, Ingmar
comes to exercise considerable influence in the colony, where his
intelligence and ability to take the initiative are of great value to
the community. He starts a flour mill and other enterprises which
restore hope and courage to his countrymen, and soon the activity
of the colony comes to resemble the production model of the home
parish. Ingmar creates a Sweden in miniature, establishing a way
out of the fanaticism and self-torment he found his countrymen
immersed in. He also saves Gertrude from insanity.

At the same time, he himself is subjected to increasingly
difficult trials during his stay in the Holy Land. He develops into
a hero who in the end rescues the entire colony from a great danger,
whereupon he becomes its unofficial leader and develops an especially
cordial relationship with the founder of the colony, Mrs. Gordon.
Undoubtedly his heroic achievements contribute to his penance. But
the mission to fetch Gertrude home appears almost impossible, for
he has begun to love his wife Barbro. It appears also that his atonement is now complete. The relationships among the characters develop harmoniously. Among the colonists Gertrude has found Bo,
a man she has come to love. Thus, Ingmar is free to return to his
wife. Despite everything, then, he carries out his mission to bring
home the woman he had so grievously wronged; when he leaves,
he is accompanied by Gertrude and her fiancé.

As he prepares to leave the colony to return home, Ingmar confronts the emigrants for the last time as the respected representative
of their native parish. He now expresses the respect that those at
home hold for those of their countrymen who courageously set out
for foreign lands. The colonists, on their part, confirm their esteem
for Ingmar and their native land, but they stress at the same time
their pride and happiness over having been able to fit their lives
into a broader and more meaningful context away from the everyday
monotony of life in the Swedish countryside.

This understanding and reconciliation builds a bridge between
the home country and the land of the emigrants. Whereas the

thematic threads are resolved in the spirit of harmony, the two opposing attitudes expressed in the book are clearly revealed: the importance of being firmly rooted in one's native soil and the exciting lure of distant lands.

The last part of *Jerusalem* shows how relationships at Ingmar farm—and, accordingly, in the entire rural community—are consolidated. This comes about because, among other reasons, Ingmar's wife Barbro becomes more Ingmar-like than the Ingmarssons themselves. She loyally maintains the family traditions and fulfills all that the role of a good housewife demands. In spirit if not by birth, she is a genuine member of the powerful clan. She also possesses its typical moral qualities. It is in fact she who convinces Ingmar to travel to Jerusalem to become reconciled with Gertrude.

While her husband is in the Holy Land, Barbro goes through a kind of purgatory. Alone and scorned, she gives birth to a child and pretends that Ingmar is not the father. But when Ingmar comes home, he sets matters straight in his private life, just as he settled conditions in the colony. Reunited with his wife, he recognizes the newborn child as his own and has him baptized Ingmar. Only now can he fully take upon himself the office of the family's Big Ingmar, the leader who upholds the values of the farm and the parish. Not only has the moral code of the family once again asserted its strength, but the family's vitality is confirmed by the birth of the new child, who points the way to future generations of Ingmarssons.

The Question of Values

A question that has provoked lively discussion in connection with *Jerusalem* is what stand the author really takes: are her sympathies with the emigrants or with those who choose to stay at home behind the plow?[12] She herself has pointed out that it was the contrast between the shrewd and sensible farmers and the "wildly romantic" undertaking of the emigrants that fascinated her and became fruitful for her literary production.[13] Travel and adventure, the bold and the reformers—these always held a fascination for Lagerlöf. On the other hand, those who represent the revival usually have a streak of callousness and fanaticism. Hellgum's sect has something of the same destructive influence on the established social system as the group of cavaliers has in *Gösta Berling's Saga*. In the manuscript of *Jerusalem*, it is evident that the revival originally was clearly defined as a destructive force in the parish. This negative view of the new movement was eliminated in the printed version.[14]

Strictly speaking, the discussion about Lagerlöf's preferences is meaningless. It was not because she wanted to take a stand for or against a certain religious position that she wrote her great novel. The themes of religious revival and emigration are actually a means, an excuse to dramatize the basic questions of value which had always been her concern. The problems that she considers essential have to do with man's position with regard to moral and social imperatives, the question of how one ought to conduct oneself in relation to life itself—to social systems and individual responsibility. The theme of the revival provided her with unusually rich possibilities for bringing these vital questions to a head. This she does by constructing for her characters a series of dilemmas, which she seeks to present with as objective an analysis as possible. This objectivity, along with her habit of considering all sides of a question, lends an unusual richness to her narrative. Her technique destroys the possibility of a simple stance for or against the sectarians.

That the question of values constitutes the core of the book explains also why Ingmar, who represents the parish and not the revival, functions as the main character and why it is precisely the story of his love and guilt that is central in a work dealing with the lives of such a variety of characters. His problems form a kind of paradigm for the crises and conflicts that affect the parish in general. At the same time, Lagerlöf is able, in a dramatic way, to relate the collective course of events into Ingmar's own personal conflict. It is of no real consequence that a good many episodes in *Jerusalem* are not directly related to the fate of its hero.

With *Jerusalem,* Lagerlöf achieved the success that made her internationally famous. The reviews of Part One prompted her friend Sophie Elkan to exclaim that it was not reviews that were being written but hymns of praise.[15] Even though the second part was received with more reserve, the Jerusalem novel was regarded as a major work. Lagerlöf had now conquered the literary critics and won popular acclaim as well. In America, however, it appears that *Jerusalem* did not enjoy popular acceptance before World War I.[16]

Because she had never been completely satisfied with the second part of *Jerusalem,* Lagerlöf undertook a thorough revision before the new edition came out in 1909. She began by clearing up some of the narrative ungainliness of the first version. More interesting, however, is the fact that she changed both the tone and the overall perspective of the novel in the new edition. In the later version, the portrayal of the colony is much more positive. Here the revival movement and the emigration become part of a meaningful plan, a confirmation of how ingeniously God disposes the fate of men. The changes include the possibilities of cultivating the Holy Land and making it fruitful through irrigation systems and other measures. From an artistic standpoint, however, it could be argued that the revisions were a change for the worse. The oppressive weightiness so effective in the first edition has disappeared.[17]

Evidently, Lagerlöf found working on *Jerusalem* both arduous and absorbing. She explained to her publisher in September of 1902 that her "thoughts, which have revolved around this book for almost three years now, appear not to want to leave it, but only to change and improve it." The letters from the *Jerusalem* period, however, do not exude the enthusiasm that at times marks the correspondence of the period when she was working on *Gösta Berling's Saga*. Then, she was just discovering, to her own surprise, her powers of creative imagination, as well as her ability to construct a story. Ten years later, she confirms the continued existence of her unusual talents with a sober self-awareness. This she does in a letter to her friend Valborg Olander in a passage that can be regarded as the ultimate insight she gained from her experience of writing *Jerusalem:*

I have, of course, considerable talent. It is not worth making a fuss over, but it is precisely because of it that my soul is in constant hunger, and it needs all the tension of this demanding work in order to find peace. (18 January 1903)

In the same matter-of-fact way, she points out her importance for the impoverished tradition of Swedish prose. She writes to another friend that she has now reached a point in her art at which she believes she can see "the possibility of really approaching something great":

Perhaps it is true, too, that the writing of novels is not so cultivated in our country, and that we have yet to do something perfect, but still I will have brought the art a great step forward before I am finished. (28 January 1903)

Lagerlöf's next major work was a book for children. Here too, she makes use of bipolar tensions that dominate *Jerusalem:* the contrast between the home and the way out.

Chapter Four

Nils Holgersson
Flies over the World

Idea and Material

None of Selma Lagerlöf's books has become as well known, both throughout the world and by generations of Swedes, as *Nils Holgerssons underbara resa genom Sverige (The Wonderful Adventures of Nils,* 1906–7). The story of a lilliputian who flies through the air over Sweden on the back of a goose has held a special fascination, particularly, it seems, for readers in countries far distant from Sweden, such as Japan and China (a Chinese translation of the book appeared as late as 1980). Very soon after it was published in Sweden, *The Wonderful Adventures of Nils* was translated into both English and German. It has also been filmed.

The book was originally commissioned for Swedish schools by the Swedish National Teachers' Society. At the turn of the century, the aim was to enable children to read works of Sweden's foremost writers. The teachers suggested to Lagerlöf that she write a book about the geography of Sweden. Feeling this to be a great responsibility, she approached the task with highest ambitions. "I want this to be one of my best books," she wrote on 22 November 1901 to Alfred Dalin, who handled negotiations between her and the Society.

Lagerlöf was already acquainted with some parts of Sweden, and in her books she had brought vividly to life various Swedish milieus. For the new project, she was forced to extend her knowledge to include the entire country. She began with the same documentary method she had used in *Jerusalem.* Much material was collected for her from different parts of the country: facts about the natural environment, cultural and historical notes, tales and legends, and, as she expressed it in the letter to Dalin, "stories of people who had performed grand or noteworthy or characteristic deeds." Finally, she undertook a special journey to Norrland, the northernmost of the three main regions of Sweden, in order to get an impression of the environment. The task at hand was to describe the country, devoting a reasonably fair amount of discussion to each of its districts. Lagerlöf, as it later turned out, would not be able to escape criticism from certain displeased provinces. [1]

Those who commissioned the book expected a collection of separate tales from different parts of Sweden. But for Lagerlöf, a writer with a love for continuity, the book had to have a unifying idea that could give schoolchildren a feeling of completeness, purpose, and excitement. To provide this, she invented the story of the boy Nils Holgersson, who travels with a flock of wild geese on a journey through Sweden. As Nils discovers the world around him, the readers, following him, become acquainted with their native country. But *The Wonderful Adventures of Nils* is much more than a geography textbook. Besides being a *Bildungsroman* in terms of its hero, it is a book that fosters the general education of its young readers. It can also be called a didactic book, though it lacks, happily, the finger-wagging moral teachings associated with that type of literature.

The book is based on a pattern—typical for Lagerlöf—of guilt, repentence, and reconciliation. At the beginning, Nils, though otherwise an ordinary boy, is extraordinarily indolent and mean. He is punished for this by being banished from the human community, changed into a liliputian, and exiled to life among the animals in the wilderness.

At first it is only a question of survival for Nils, but soon his possibilities for action increase, and he becomes involved in matters that promote the betterment of both his traveling companions and his environment. Finally, he takes on the function of a hero. At this point, it is time for the author to break the spell. Nils becomes human again—a sign that the process of moral transformation has been completed.

Because its action is based on the dual foundation of myth and realism, its narrative pattern is similar to that of *Gösta Berling's Saga*. The transformation motif affords the possibility of an episodic presentation of events in the present. Anything at all can happen while Nils is on his journey with the wild geese. Concurrently, the time perspective is deepened by the narrator's dealing with what happened before the period of Nils's journey. This is accomplished

by including magical encounters between Nils and figures from
Sweden's historical and legendary past.

The Action

The action begins with the story of the transformation itself. Nils
is presented as a nasty, insufferable boy, a problem for his hard-
working parents. At the onset, the book was supposed to be aimed
at nine-year-old readers, but Lagerlöf, with an unerring sense of a
child's curiosity about slightly older children, made her main character a fourteen-year-old. In a way, *The Wonderful Adventures of Nils*
is about a puberty crisis, about the dream of escaping from all that
is dull and boring and embracing adventure, danger, and excitement. It is also, of course, about the feeling, experienced by many
during puberty, of alienation from accepted social norms.[2]

The first chapter is one of the most concentrated and exciting
that Lagerlöf has ever written. She begins according to the formula
of the fairy tale—"Once upon a time there was a boy"—thereby
signaling that anything could happen. But at the beginning everything conforms to down-to-earth reality. The reader is introduced
to a small farm in the south of Sweden on a Sunday in early spring.
Only three people live there—father, mother, and son. The parents
would be quite satisfied with their lot, were it not for their worries
about the boy, whom they scarcely can rely on to tend the geese.
On this particular Sunday, the boy has refused to accompany his
parents to church. They have given him the assignment of reading
the day's Biblical text and commentary while he is home alone, and
they intend to question him about it when they return. After poring
over Luther's *Commentary*, he succumbs to drowsiness and falls asleep.
It is now that the fantastic action begins.

When he awakens, he sees, to his surprise, a little elf in the
room. At this point, the reader is given a demonstration of the boy's
nastiness. Nils teases the imp unmercifully, taking him captive and
ignoring his pleas to be freed. But suddenly he feels a burning slap
in the face and is transformed into a *Thumbietot (tummetott)*—that
is, an imp about the size of Tom Thumb, a "little monster," a
"changeling," as Nils later calls himself on different occasions.

He is afraid to appear before people in this guise; he has, however,
acquired the ability to communicate with animals. When a young
gander on the farm heeds the enticing calls of a flock of wild geese

and flies into the air to follow them, Nils tries unsuccessfully to prevent him. Instead, he finds himself going along on their flight, becoming an unusual participant in the journey of a flock of wild geese through Sweden up to Lapland and back again toward the South.

The Journey Motif

The Wonderful Adventures of Nils continues in the solid tradition established by classic travel and adventure tales, many of which were originally written for children.[3] The motif of the flight afforded considerable narrative advantages. The geography of the country could be presented from above in easily accessible, sweeping panoramas. Fields, for example, appear as patchwork quilts or as borders on mother's apron—domestic images, as it were, that connect the story with the children's experience. For a person who never experienced air travel, Lagerlöf exhibits a manner of observation that corresponds surprisingly well with the optical perspective of air travelers of a later time.

The regions of Sweden are presented in broad outline, as the wild geese fly over them. But since the flock must stop frequently to eat and sleep, numerous occasions arise for showing detailed pictures of the vegetation, the industry, and the culture of various places. In this way, Lagerlöf achieves a double perspective. It is precisely this double perspective that Czeslaw Milosz praises her for in his 1980 Nobel Lecture; specifically, he cites it as a work that "influenced, to a large extent . . . [his] notions of poetry," and speaks of its hero "who flies above the earth and looks at it *from above* but at the same time sees it in every detail." "This double vision," Milosz believes, "may be a metaphor of the poet's vocation": a combination of "avidity of the eye" for the large picture and the endeavor to describe in detail what is seen.

The Figures

As is customary in the fictional world of Lagerlöf, the story of Nils Holgersson acquaints the reader with many characters. The wild geese form a core group of figures, similar to the cavaliers in *Gösta Berling's Saga*. Interacting with the geese is a series of secondary figures, each of them a significant personality: the eagle Gorgo, the raven Bataki, the stork Herr Ermenrich, and the moose Grayfell.

Smirre the fox, the villain of the drama (somewhat reminiscent of Sintram in *Gösta Berling's Saga*) creates a suspenseful atmosphere throughout much of the story by threatening and pursuing the wild geese, who, of course, always succeed in tricking him.

While Lagerlöf took the idea of having a child grow up among animals with human qualities from Kipling's *The Jungle Books* (1894 and 1895), the similarities between the works scarcely extend beyond this main idea.[4] The atmosphere in the two works differs considerably. In *The Wonderful Adventures of Nils,* the reader enters into a typical Lagerlöf world, where the lead goose Akka resembles the imperious Major's Wife of *Gösta Berling's Saga* or the authoritative Ingmar Ingmarsson of *Jerusalem.*

Both on land and in the air, social and psychological dramas are played—the battles, disputes, and decisions of animals, as well as the beautiful love story of Nils's friend the gander and a young female goose, Dunfin. In this interplay of feelings and conflicts, Nils gradually assumes an increasingly important role. His contribution to the flock is reminiscent of what Ingmar Ingmarsson does for the colony in *Jerusalem.* Nils becomes indispensable for the geese, especially for his help in protecting his friends against Smirre the fox.

As counterpart and complement to Nils and his journey through the air, the story includes two other wayfaring children, Osa goose-girl and her little brother Mats. They travel in the same direction as Nils flies, and now and then their paths cross with those of the imp, who helps and protects them.

It is important for the readers to meet a few "real" children with both feet on the ground, who arouse sympathy and admiration. Osa goose-girl and little Mats are abandoned children, plagued by misfortune. Their mother had died of tuberculosis, and their father had simply disappeared. They travel around in search of their father— a motif with a long tradition in literature, going back as far as the search of Telemachus for Odysseus in *The Odyssey.* At the same time, these children serve a concrete, didactic purpose: they educate the readers about tuberculosis, the disease that destroyed their family, and inform people about hygiene and other practical measures for avoiding contagion.

It is noteworthy that Lagerlöf does not include in her book any rosy-cheeked, model children for readers to identify with. An interest in children who do not fare well in the adult world is often predominant in her works. In *Gösta Berling's Saga*, the daughter of the clergyman from Broby never gets enough to eat because her father is so stingy. In *The Miracles of Antichrist*, Lagerlöf describes child laborers in the mines of Italy. *The Tale of a Manor, The Balloon, Thy Soul Shall Bear Witness*, and *Anna Svärd*—all are examples of stories in which children are ill-treated.

In *The Wonderful Adventures of Nils*, the main purpose of which was to give children "an amicable, beautiful picture of their country" (letter to Dalin, 22 November 1901), Osa goose-girl and Mats manage to get along rather well in spite of everything by making themselves useful to adults, carrying out their orders and running their errands. Their lot is certainly a hard one, but they illustrate one of the main points of the story—that people can cope with even the most difficult circumstances. In one instance, this idea is expressed with almost American optimism: "Even today, cleverness and competence can change a beggar into a prince."

From the standpoint of sexual roles, it is not insignificant that the smartest and most courageous character in the story is a girl. Osa goose-girl is a young counterpart of Akka, the leader of the flock. When the wayfaring children reach Lapland and little Mats dies suddenly as the result of an accident, his sister develops into a genuine heroine. She has to convince the most powerful man in the locality, the director of mines, that Mats is worthy of a respectable funeral. The director is moved by her words of praise in memory of her brother, and he gives her his support. Lagerlöf often depicted burials and funeral processions, scenes that had considerably greater significance in the agrarian Sweden of her day than they do now. She even regarded the story of little Mats's funeral as the high point in the second part of the book.[5] The motif shows her deep respect for the child.

Osa's wanderings end when she finally finds her father, an adult upon whom she can depend; now she can once again be the child she has a right to be. Lagerlöf's view of the adult-child relationship is clear: children are capable of much, but the responsibility must be borne by adults.

Social Message and Moral

The Wonderful Adventures of Nils provides the reader with a wealth of knowledge about the natural and social environment of Sweden.

The book also gives a sampling of the problems that people had to struggle with at the time: emigration to America, poverty, and tuberculosis. Special questions are taken up, such as draining of lakes, forestry, and prevention of cruelty to animals. Surprisingly, much is still current; in fact, some of the ecological questions that Lagerlöf was concerned about have become even more acute. Without minimizing the difficulties and anxieties of existence, the book conveys an optimistic message. In contrast to Strindberg, for example, Lagerlöf is convinced of the importance of industrialization for the country's prosperity. Her story is deeply rooted in "places where contemporary life is flourishing richly and powerfully" (letter to Dalin, 22 November 1901), and it shows the possibilities for advancement through hard work, good will, and solidarity. She embraces the concept that, in Swedish politics, later came to be known as the *folkhemsidé,* or the idea of the People's Home—the notion that the state ought to function as a good home in which everyone contributes to its growth and development.

On the other hand, it would be anachronistic to expect of Lagerlöf a modern view of equality. As in her other books, people are assigned different roles at work and in society. King Oscar II reigns over all—he even intervenes as a deus ex machina in one of the episodes of the book. His elevated position is brought out by the fact that he alone speaks in the plural, whereas the other figures in the book use singular forms in their dialogues. The director of mines in Lapland—a character based on a person Lagerlöf met on her trip to Norrland—also plays an important and decisive role. His patriarchal influence balances Akka's female leadership of the world of the birds. Lagerlöf had originally planned to have a male lead goose, but came later to think better of it.

It is decisive for Lagerlöf's view of humanity that every person in his or her calling has merit and responsibility. Herein lies the book's greatest social significance. An important example of this idea is the description of a woman from Dalecarlia, her hard life and many jobs. It is designed as a tribute to the anonymous workers in an impoverished Sweden. The ideal representative of the country is the Swedish farmer. He is shown as the very model of industriousness, symbolizing honor and diligence, the same qualities possessed by the sons of Ingmar in *Jerusalem.*

The Wonderful Adventures of Nils is a book that not only provides information; it also imparts certain social and moral values to its readers. One social phenomenon stands out as absolutely negative—the emigration to America. While working on the book, Lagerlöf wrote, "Through my reader, I want the young people to get an accurate picture of their country and to learn to love and understand it; I want them also to learn something about its many resources and the possibilities for development that it offers, so that they won't dash off to America at the first temptation" (letter to Josepha Ahnfeldt, 18 November 1904). One episode in the book becomes especially stamped in the readers' consciousness—the story of a sick old farm woman whose cow, unfed and unmilked, lows in the barn. The woman is dying, and she has no one to console her on her deathbed or to continue her work on the farm, for her children have deserted her. They have all emigrated to America. This scene is an admonishment to the schoolchildren of Sweden not to forsake their native land. It also contains the message, typical for the times, that children should remember that they are responsible for their aging parents. In 1910, every fifth Swede lived in America, and children's literature was especially packed with propaganda against emigration. When Lagerlöf was not writing for children, however, her attitude toward emigration was sympathetic; for example, in her speech for women's suffrage in 1911, "Home and State," she equates the emancipation of women with the wave of emigration, precisely in order to show how necessary women's emancipation is.

The story of Nils Holgersson also sets up positive models for the good life. In the chapter "A Little Farm," Lagerlöf introduces her own childhood home as a model for ideal existence. The people there lived simply and unpretentiously, but their life was good because it consisted of a harmonious union of work and pleasure. A well-ordered home life represents one pole in Lagerlöf's concept of what life ought to be. The other is the desire for adventure and new experiences. Nils's flight with the geese and the experience of ever-new landscapes are stimulating features of the story, as well as the description of the radiance of the sun and the beauty of nature in contrast to the darkness of the forest and the fear brought on by nightfall. From the beginning of her career as a writer, motion was fundamental to Lagerlöf. She always regarded traveling most favorably. As she expresses it in *The Wonderful Adventures of Nils,* "The world is wonderful to live in, both for small and big people. It is also a good thing to be free and without cares and to have the whole world open before you."

Lagerlöf's novel about Nils Holgersson is a *Bildungsroman,* in which the protagonist is changed by his experiences. Its pedagogical pattern is a direct outgrowth of the adventures the boy experiences. Although there is nothing pedantic about the novel, certain virtues do stand out as absolute: under no circumstances can one break a promise or resort to violence to achieve a goal. Gratitude, loyalty, and mercy are brought home as moral imperatives, and primary importance is placed upon generosity in communal and personal relationships. Love and concern for his fellow beings are what enable Nils to overcome his egoism and become helpful to others. At first his consideration does not extend beyond the white gander, his only close acquaintance in the strange animal world, but it soon reaches out to the wild geese and to the animals not connected with the flock. Even Smirre the fox, the enemy of the wild geese, is finally conceded a tolerable existence through the efforts of Nils. As an imp, Nils gradually dares to take on the most difficult feats. He is especially good at filing the bars of cages in order to free captive birds. The acknowledgement of his good deeds comes in the form of the favor of Mother Akka, his moral authority.

Thus on his long journey, Nils learns the art of communal living. At the same time, he realizes his own identity. The change that takes place in him is expressed even in the body language of the old and the new Nils. In the penultimate chapter of the book, when Nils has just been changed into a human being and reunited with his parents, we read, "The Nils Holgersson who went away last spring had a heavy and slow gait and slow speech and sleepy eyes, but this one who returned was light and nimble and spoke quickly, and he had eyes that shone and sparkled."

The Novel as a Book for Children

Much has been written about *The Wonderful Adventures of Nils,* but little about the book as a story for children. Quantitatively, the story covers enough pages to fill perhaps ten ordinary children's books; it is the most monumental story ever written for young people. In what way has Lagerlöf striven to appeal to her child audience? Properly speaking, there is no special attempt to cater to children in the book. It is being crafted on an adult level. The children are introduced to adult life in a manner that many today hold up as desirable. Since the young readers are called upon to take responsibility for the future, they must participate in the experiences of adults and submit to their values. In this respect, the story is not childish. An important symbolism lies in the fact that Nils remains diminutive up to the point at which he acquires the norms of the adult world. Only then does he become the size of a normal human being again.

But Lagerlöf did indeed take pains to appeal to children. The lilliputian perspective itself is typical of children's stories, probably because it affords the opportunity to characterize the alienation of children in the world of adults. The well-known fondness of children for animal characters was surely a major reason for the story being rooted in a world other than one inhabited exclusively by humans. Animals who talk and act like human beings belong essentially to the ancient genres of the saga and the fable, which, however, were not primarily intended for children.

In her narrative technique, Lagerlöf aims above all at clarity and lively depiction. Surprises and sudden changes occur incessantly in the story, but they are balanced by meticulous preparation for, and development of, all that takes place. This preparatory technique is an important trait in the narration. The arrival in a new region is preceded by a detailed introduction or by tales, dreams, or other types of allegories. Another method the author employs is to describe first places and types of vegetation and then have Nils speculate about what the landscape under him really is like—a piece of cloth, for example, or a leaf. In his fantasy, Nils projects himself beyond the realm of reality, as a child in the schoolroom can be tempted to fantasize beyond the subject at hand or to seek after further knowledge. Another important feature of the story is repetition, which often lends the work a formulaic character. Repeated phrases, pauses, moments in which the message is brought home—all these structure the story for the reader.

Lagerlöf also devoted considerable care to the level of language in *The Wonderful Adventures of Nils;* in fact, she enlisted the help of experts in determining the language of the book. In no way does one get the impression that the language is that of children. Nils, Osa goose-girl, and little Mats all speak like adults. Paradoxically, the work appears in some instances to be more difficult than certain of Lagerlöf's books for adults. This stems from the fact that the author often assumes a naive tone in her other works; for example, she has a child determine the perspective in *Gösta Berling's Saga,* as she does in the beginning of *Jerusalem* and *The Miracles of Antichrist,* in *Liliecrona's Home,* and in the Mårbacka books. The small tenant farmer's perspective in *The Emperor of Portugallia* is also highly naive. In *The Wonderful Adventures of Nils,* Lagerlöf clearly avoids having Nils's own language or perspective narrow the horizon. At the same time, however, she simplifies Swedish prose by eliminating the plural forms in the colloquial language and by modernizing the spelling. The syntax is plain and clear, with main clauses dominating.

When Lagerlöf began work on her geography of Sweden, she was concerned primarily with the didactic aspects of the project. She knew that children are critical readers, and she was careful not to make any factual errors. Yet a good many so-called experts came down on her when the book was published. She herself conceded confidentially (in a letter to Dalin) that some criticism of zoological points was valid, but that much of it was mere nit-picking.

On the whole, the book was received with exuberant praise and regarded as a valuable gift for children. But there was criticism not only of the factual materials but also of the ideology and the language. Some thought that Nils enjoyed himself too much on his journey and that that could entice children to daydream in school. While Lagerlöf previously had used fantasy as a means of approaching geographical and psychological reality without being faulted for it (she had done this, for example, in *Gösta Berling's Saga*), she drew criticism for blending a "fairy tale" with the depiction of reality in a book for children. This negative evaluation stemmed from the notion that the fantastical features could confuse the facts and lead the children on the wrong path.[6] At the turn of the century, however, pedagogues were beginning to believe that feelings and fantasy were the most important channels through which morals and knowledge could be acquired.

In *The Wonderful Adventures of Nils,* as in Swift's *Gulliver's Travels,* fantasy is a springboard for realism. Milieus, dimensions, explanations, cause-and-effect relationships—all have a precise realistic quality. As Gunnar Ahlström wrote in his excellent monograph on Lagerlöf's novel, "With her paradoxical work of art, Selma Lagerlöf succeeded in writing an incredible fairy tale in such a way that it appeals to the readers' sense of familiarity and sense of reality."[7]

Lagerlöf did not write any more books for children, apparently because she feared being classified as an author of children's books. When she refused requests to continue her successful career as a children's author, she stressed that she had to write books in which she did not need to concern herself with anything other than literary qualities.[8]

Chapter Five
Short Fiction: The Short Stories, Legends, and Short Novels

Types of Short Stories

Throughout her literary career, Lagerlöf wrote many short narrative works, a number of which were commissioned for newspapers and journals. She especially had many requests to contribute stories to Christmas editions of newspapers, which explains why many of her short stories concern winter and the celebration of Christmas. Lagerlöf was extremely conscientious when it came to these occasional pieces, and some of her Christmas stories, such as "The Peace of God" and "The Legend of the Christmas Roses" ("Legenden om julrosorna"), have become minor classics in Sweden.

Lagerlöf's first collection of short stories, *Invisible Links* (1894), established her as a writer of short fiction. The collection came out in several editions, augmented in 1904 by additional short pieces that she wrote in the closing years of the 1890s, some of which are counted among her finest works. Lagerlöf's publisher, Bonniers, also decided to publish collections of her short stories, reminiscences, and speeches in the interludes between the publication of her longer novels. In 1908, *The Girl from the Marshcroft (En saga om en saga och andra sagor)* was published, followed by the first part of *Troll och människor (Trolls and Men)* in 1915 and the second part in 1921. An additional collection of short prose, *Höst (Harvest)* came out in 1933. The final collection was a two-volume posthumous edition, *Från skilda tider 1943–1945*, which contains many short stories from various periods in Lagerlöf's literary career.[1]

Frequently, a short story reveals a more intimate picture of its author than does a long novel. This can be said of Lagerlöf's stories, which reflect the great range of her talent and present a variety of structures and styles. Her short stories are more experimental than her longer works, in which the plot often dominates the entire work in an explicit way. For the most part, Lagerlöf's short stories are based on anecdotes or other clear and simple narratives. She works in a tradition in which the narrative concludes with a point, or a solution to the psychological problem that lies at the core of the story. Sometimes she strives to achieve a light style in the spirit of Maupassant, but these stories are not especially successful. On the other hand, she works extremely well within the model of the fairy tale and folktale, and she is also a master of the legend.

A line of development can be seen in her short prose works—from a narrative overloaded with symbols into a concentrated structure in which each word is carefully weighed. During an early period, she succumbed to a "mania for description" in the manner of the Danish symbolist Jens Peter Jacobsen,[2] as can be seen in "Stenkumlet" ("The King's Grave") in *Osynliga länkar (Invisible Links)*, a story with a number of visual elements, including the color red as a dominant symbol for the ruthless affirmation of life, as opposed to the acceptance of limits and responsibilities. A half-ruined cairn, the grave of a king, takes on the same fateful function as the famous millrace in Ibsen's *Rosmersholm;* Ibsen was, of course, an inevitable model for the symbolists of the 1890s.[3]

Gradually, however, Lagerlöf's short fiction became oriented toward other models. The Icelandic saga and the works of Bjørnson and Jensen influenced her in developing a more concise form. Both the short stories and the fairy- and folk tales came to concentrate more directly on the action, with some of the later ones becoming almost expressionistic. Then, considerable tension arises from the discrepancy between the surface structure of a narrative and its deeper meaning.

Lagerlöf's short stories present a whole cavalcade of people: farmers and crofters, cavaliers and men of property, clergymen and beautiful girls, old people about to meet death, saints and murderers. She seems to understand them all and to be capable of interpreting their secrets, whether those secrets concern the sacrificial ardour of the saint or the hatefulness of the sadist.

In her short stories, Lagerlöf often depicts a person who has reached a turning point in life. Since guilt and responsibility are such essential problems in her writing, the moment is often one of enquiry or examination. The short story may be written in a lyrical

vein, but at the same time it is dramatically effective in its focus
on drastic change, the choice of path. The resolution usually takes
the form of absolute happiness or tragic ruin.

Lagerlöf wrote contemporary short stories, historical narratives,
and stories not bound to any particular time. While she often deals
with contemporary social themes, it is clear that, like many other
writers, she felt that she had greater freedom when writing from a
historical perspective. She was particularly interested in the period
of transition from paganism to Christianity in Sweden, and she
included themes from this period in the stories "De fågelfria" ("The
Outlaws"), "Stenkumlet" ("The King's Grave"), and "Reors saga"
("The Legend of Reor"), as well as in the stories in the collection
Drottningar i Kungahälla (The Queens of Kungahälla). Her materials
came from various literary sources, primarily Snorri's Heimskringla,
which had been her favorite reading since childhood.

Set in various provinces of Sweden, Lagerlöf's short stories attest
to her ability to create both historical and geographical authenticity.
Several of the earlier stories are connected with Bohuslän, a western
province she became familiar with when she visited her brother, a
doctor in the small southern Bohuslän city of Kungälv. Another
group of stories is set in the island of Gotland, Sweden's eastern
outpost, which she visited during the 1890s, as did many other
artists and writers of the period. Traces of her journeys abroad can
also be seen in the stories set in Italy,[4] the Near East, and other
places. Of greatest importance, however, are the stories set in Värmland, with Lagerlöf's home district, often called Svartsjö, at the
center. Several stories tell of what happens to the individual cavaliers
from Gösta Berling's Saga after they leave the joyous life at Ekeby,
while others, such as "Gravskriften" ("The Epitaph") and "Bröd-
erna" ("The Brothers"), depict the problems of village folk, with
the entire district as background.

In stories resembling folk tales or legends, the place names are
especially important, for such tales are always rooted in a definite
locale. Stories such as En herrgårdssägen (The Tale of a Manor), "Tom-
ten på Töreby" ("The Imp at Töreby"), and "Sankta Katarina av
Siena" ("Saint Catherine of Siena") suggest by their very titles how
important the setting is for the action. Lagerlöf belongs to those
writers who with only a few details can create a memorable picture
of a region, often integrating scenic depiction with psychological
motifs. She often introduces a short story with a description of the

setting that includes symbolic elements; the landscape thus fore-shadows and accompanies the psychological problems of the story. This technique can be seen in "The Epitaph" and "En historia från Halstanäs" ("The Story of Halstanäs"), both of which appear in the collection *Invisible Links.*

Fairy-Tale Structure

In some of her short pieces that could be classified as fairy tales, Lagerlöf, in keeping with the demands of the fairy tales, avoids designating the exact geographical location of the action. Nor does she limit these stories with regard to time. She begins many of them with the fairy-tale formula, "Once upon a time" or, more often, with "There was," thereby allowing herself the maximum freedom in re-creating a time and a place. This is the pattern she follows in stories such as "The Peace of God" and "The Sons of Ingmar," the narratives she incorporated into *Jerusalem.* They were not connected with either Dalecarlia or any specific time, which enables her to place the greatest emphasis on the moral problems her characters are involved in.[5]

The fairy-tale genre arouses special expectations of excitement, suspense, and fantasy, all of which Lagerlöf's stories provide. But despite the fact that she is so often called a teller of fairy tales, she does not merely relate fantasy-filled stories; indeed, she very rarely writes what would be considered genuine fairy tales. She uses, rather, the method of the fairy tale as a basis for organizing a story. She is most successful when she strives to create the suspense and mystery characteristic of the fairy tale. She often builds her action according to the three-step rule and employs the matter-of-fact style typical of the fairy tale. This holds true even in situations such as fateful encounters between persons or between man and nature. She uses upheaval, surprise, and metamorphosis in a way that can be associated with the fairy tale. The successful solution to the problem that the fairy tale usually presents is also typical of many of her stories. Complete unity between man and nature, blurring the distinction between fantasy and reality—all this is characteristic of Lagerlöf's short tales. While these traits are also found in some of her other works, they often appear in a purer form in the short stories. The very title of one of her collections, *Trolls and Men,* illustrates this union of the real and the fantastic.

Lagerlöf uses the fairy-tale genre both freely and artfully. By adopting the method of the fairy tale, she achieves naive effects, but the psychology is far more complex. "Bortbytingen" ("The Changeling," 1908), published in *Trolls and Men,* is an excellent example of a story patterned after a folk legend but with a modern psychological meaning; it is actually an allegory of a marriage on the verge of breaking up because the mother is completely occupied with the child. The changeling motif in both fairy and folktales goes back to a popular fear that an infant would be exchanged for a troll child if its mother did not take special precautions, a notion that explains in folk superstition why some children are born deformed. Tales of changelings usually are concerned with how the kidnapped child lives among the trolls. Lagerlöf, however, reverses the motif, depicting instead a troll in the world of men. While traveling on horseback with her husband, a farmer's wife loses her infant child, who is stolen by an old troll woman. When the parents desperately look for the child, they find instead an ugly troll child, with claws and a tail. The wife takes it home with her and looks after it with the greatest care and attention. Her husband protests, but not even his threats to leave home keep his wife from fulfilling her difficult task of caring for the repulsive troll. In the end, the conflict is resolved in the harmonious manner typical of the fairy tale. When the situation appears to be hopeless, the husband and wife get their beautiful, fair-haired little boy back again. The woman's sacrifices not only helped the child to survive in the world of the trolls, but also brought about its release. The husband returns home with his son in his arms (where the troll child goes is not mentioned).[6]

Folktale Structure

Lagerlöf's knowledge of folktales was of great importance for her short fiction, for she frequently employs its typical form, adhering to it stringently.[7] In contrast to the fairy tale, which typically aims at a happy ending, the folktale usually has a tragic conclusion. The short stories of Lagerlöf most consistently based on folktale motifs deal most often with crime and punishment and sometimes evince a fascination for violence. "The Outlaws," "Tale Thott," and "The Story of Halstanäs" (all in *Invisible Links*), which are based on folktale motifs, are stories of criminals. And "The Imp at Töreby," "Vattnet

i Kyrkviken" ("The Water in Kyrkviken"), and "Gammal fäbod-
sägen" ("The Tale of the Old Saeter")—all in *Trolls and Men*—end
in horror. In all these stories, the idea of nemesis predominates,
with human pride appearing to call forth, or contribute to, misfortune and unhappiness.

There are several different kinds of folktales. Among these is the
ghost story, Lagerlöf's favorite type since the days when she experienced it, with all its terror-struck fascination, in the nursery at
Mårbacka. As a teacher, she often told ghost stories to her pupils,
something that was not always appreciated by school officials.[8] Her
first literary attempt at a ghost story was "Karln" ("The Man"),
which was rejected for publication when she wrote it but published
posthumously.[9] She later took up the theme of "The Man" in one
of her most clearly defined ghost stories, *Löwensköldska ringen (The
Ring of the Löwenskölds)*, a short novel written in 1925.

Along with the gloomy narratives that show man at the mercy
of the powers, there are also stories of a different kind, impression-
istic sketches which point up the irony of life and love stories.
Elements of both these genres are found in one of Lagerlöf's most
beloved short stories, "Dunungen" ("Downie") in *Invisible Links*,[10]
a love story with a comic tone, narrated somewhat in the style of
Hans Christian Andersen. Lagerlöf herself wrote a dramatization of
the story, which was later filmed.

A frequent theme, especially in the early stories, is the struggle
of the individual to find his way in a chaotic situation. In the
narratives, as in *Gösta Berling's Saga*, passion is pitted against moral
imperatives. The motif of sin and atonement is varied in connection
with the problems that revolve around determinism and responsibility. The question of the extent of man's possibilities for mastering
his own destiny occurs again and again in Lagerlöf's works.

The main character in a Lagerlöf short story is often a socially or
psychologically disadvantaged person. In her earlier stories, man is
often defeated in his struggle, but gradually the tone of her narratives
becomes more optimistic, with the author presenting characters
whose power and strength of will bring them to reconciliation. "The
Wedding March" (in *The Girl from the Marshcroft*) exemplifies this
optimism. The story deals with a poor violinist who does not enjoy
public recognition, despite his indisputable genius. Ultimately it
relates how fame comes to him and, above all, how his artistry
influences those around him.[11]

In some of the short stories, there are women who find their destiny through having been neglected. The Cinderella motif is, for example, the basic theme in "Downie," in which a tender, delicate young girl makes a courageous choice in the end, as well as in *The Girl from the Marshcroft,* in which a poor tenant farm girl marries a rich farmer. "The Epitaph" depicts a woman who is at first weak and submissive, but who finally asserts the right to her own feelings.[12]

The Queens of Kungahälla

While their multiplicity of themes and forms make the collections of Lagerlöf's short stories fascinating, the author herself preferred to publish collections with a unified subject matter and a consistent theme. *Drottningar i Kungahälla (The Queens of Kungahälla,* 1899) is an example of such a collection. It tells of the Swedish queens of the Viking period who celebrated their weddings in the city of Kungahälla, the present-day Kungälv, near the border between Sweden and Norway. In this period of transition, there were frequent battles between the Nordic countries, and as Christianity began to drive out paganism, the religious and political complications increased. Lagerlöf, who found these conflicts fascinating, became well acquainted with the history and topography of Kungälv when she visited the city in the 1890s, just when an interesting archeological discovery had been made there.[13] Her stories about the women who celebrated or wanted to celebrate their weddings in the city have a historical basis. *The Queens of Kungahälla* can be seen as a bold attempt to create a feminist counterpart to Snorri Sturluson's history of the kings of Norway, *Heimskringla.*

The purpose of this collection of short stories was also to describe different types of women, something in which Lagerlöf had already excelled in *Gösta Berling's Saga.* One encounters in these stories refined women and good women, dangerous women, and women with a zest for living. The longest story, entitled "Astrid," is one of mistaken identity, in which the title character, with craftiness and cunning, manages to get the husband she wants, Olaf, who was destined to become St. Olaf. Contrasting with Astrid is her half sister, the mild and saintly Ingegärd, who actually from the very beginning had been the one designated to marry Olaf.

Elements of the legend are strong in several of the short stories in *The Queens of Kungahälla,* as, for example, in the story in which

Olaf Tryggvason rejects the pagan queen Sigrid Storråda. In a dream vision, he sees how his insult to the Swedish queen brings about his martyr's death. Margareta Fredkulla, in the story of the same title, is transformed by the pressure of circumstances into a saint. For the sake of peace and her impoverished people, she sacrifices herself, overcoming her aversion to the bellicose and faithless bridegroom who awaits her.

Legends

When *The Queens of Kungahälla* was published in 1899, the volume included a group of stories designated as legends and given the simple title *Legender (Legends)*. In 1906, these legends appeared in a single volume. Two years earlier, in 1904, *Kristuslegender (Christ Legends)* was published, which together with *Legends* contain Lagerlöf's most important work in that genre.

Elements of the legend appear, however, as early as *Gösta Berling's Saga,* and they are common in the later novels, especially *The Miracles of Antichrist, Jerusalem II* (or *The Holy City*), and *The Emperor of Portugallia*. As early as 1892, the journal *Ord och bild* published "Legenden om fågelboet" ("The Legend of the Bird's Nest") in which a hardened, vengeful hermit is changed into a mild man resembling St. Francis of Assisi, who stands with upstretched arms to give the birds a haven in the wilderness. Lagerlöf's legends grew out of her strong interest in inner changes or conversions—transformations that frequently occur as miracles in her stories.

The legend is a genre difficult to define. Though it is close to the folktale and has its beginnings in pre-Christian times, it flourished especially during the late Middle Ages. At the end of the nineteenth century, the symbolists became interested in the legend form, seeing in it possibilities for describing religious experiences and elusive psychological phenomena. Around the turn of the century, the legend became Lagerlöf's most important medium for literary expression, evidenced by the fact that she wrote at least one legend a year between 1894 and 1906.[14]

It was during her first journey to Italy, in 1895–96, that Lagerlöf developed her actual passion for the legend. She had, in a sense, entered into the world of the legend, and she eagerly collected material, especially popular anecdotes related to cloisters and churches in Catholic Europe. She also became acquainted with research being done on the legend, primarily with works on Sicilian folklore by the Italian scholar Giuseppe Pitré.

There are two main types of legends—stories of the lives of saints and stories related to the folktale. Lagerlöf wrote several saints' legends—"Saint Catherine of Siena," "Lucia," and "Ljuslågan" ("The Light of the Flame"), for example, but most of her legends are closer to the folktale. One of her plans was to write a series of legends linked with cities in Italy. Two that arose out of this project are "Fiskarringen" ("The Ring of the Fisherman"), set in Venice, and "Den heliga bilden i Lucca" ("The Legend of the Sacred Image"). The stress in these stories, however, is placed not on the local but on the psychological dynamics. In "The Legend of the Sacred Image," for example, Lagerlöf discusses the naive trust that provides the requisite basis for the miracle.

After the Italian legends, Lagerlöf, strongly inspired by her visit to the Near East in 1899–1900, approached the world of legends connected with the Holy Land. For *Christ Legends,* which she characterized alternately as a book for children and a popular book, she gathered material on the childhood of Jesus from the apocryphal Gospels, as well as from several other sources, including Giuseppe Pitré's work *Fiabe e leggende popolari siciliane.* The *Christ Legends* have a more naive character than her earlier legends; the nucleus of each story is a miracle which is left unexplained, as is often the case in saints' legends proper.

Jesus is described as a normal child, full of life, whose unlimited trust and affection dominate the stories. In perfectly narrated episodes, the simple, concrete events of Jesus' childhood are told—his birth (the miracle of which is described from three different points of view), the impending danger from Herod, the flight to Egypt, and the visit to the temple when he was twelve years old. Last in the series is the complicated legend of St. Veronica's veil, which culminates in Jesus making his way to the cross.

Lagerlöf gradually became an expert on legends. She restored and adapted them, and she expanded them with additional levels of meaning. As the scholar Gunnel Weidel notes, "none of her legends bear the guise of the simple, objective narratives characteristic of medieval legends."[15] Lagerlöf did, however, possess the ability to evoke a biblical or medieval atmosphere while at the same time creating characters whose problems appear real to the modern reader. Characteristic of the legend is its naive and almost idyllic atmosphere, in which the miraculous appears to occur naturally. In Lagerlöf's legends, the introduction of the miracle into the everyday world in a manner that is both shocking and, at the same time, quite natural is central to her narrative technique.

Several years ago in an interview, the Nobel Prize–winning Swedish writer Harry Martinson stated that he believed it was unfortunate that Lagerlöf devoted herself so intensely to the genre of the legend.[16] Her contemporary critics, though, would scarcely have agreed. The critic Oscar Levertin advised her to remain in the forests of her fairy tales and the cities of her legends.[17]

Later scholars have pointed out the contradiction between the skeptical Lagerlöf, well schooled in the natural sciences, and the author of the naive narrative stance. For Lagerlöf, the legend was an aesthetically fruitful form, not a religious statement. The legend was also a means of reaching many people. It was through that genre that she seriously gained the acceptance of an international public, especially in Catholic countries. According to one critic, it was with the legend that she "most strongly approached an international and universally human wave length," because "the themes she treats in her legends are no longer the exclusive heritage of her national homeland, but a common cultural heritage for peoples of all countries."[18]

The Short Novels

During various periods of her literary career, Lagerlöf wrote several pieces of short fiction with a format different from that of her usual short stories; these can be classified as long short stories or short novels. To this group belong *En herrgårdssägen (The Tale of a Manor)*, *Herr Arnes penningar (The Treasure,* also translated as *Herr Arne's Hoard)*, *Tösen från Stormyrtorpet (The Girl from the Marshcroft)*, and *Löwensköldska ringen (The Ring of the Löwenskölds)*. *Körkarlen (Thy Soul Shall Bear Witness)* can also be included in this group, even though it is a more voluminous work. Artistically these works, written with an unusual command of narrative technique, belong to the best of Lagerlöf's oeuvre. Although the stories present many characters, they still cannot be considered collective novels, as are *Gösta Berling's Saga* and *Jerusalem*. For the most part, the action takes place in the borderland between dream and reality. The stories are based on the fairy-tale and folktale structure, and they contain striking symbolic elements, mostly from the realm of nature mysticism. They are also marked by psychological realism.[19]

At the center of each story is a young girl who experiences great suffering for the sake of love. This is true of Ingrid in *The Tale of a Manor*, Elsalill in *The Treasure*, Helga in *The Girl from the Marshcroft*, Edith in *Thy Soul Shall Bear Witness*, and Marit in *The Ring of the Löwenskölds*. All these girls, who are willing to make great sacrifices, have to face a hard social reality. At the same time, they represent love and spiritual life. Their stories have a basis in Lagerlöf's own fantasies of sacrificing her happiness for the love of a student, as reported later in *The Diary of Selma Lagerlöf*.

The Treasure

Of all the short novels, *The Treasure* achieves the highest degree of literary excellence. It is a story with clear contours. Its harsh language, influenced by Icelandic literature, is occasionally tempered by lyrical accents and Biblical rhetoric. The story takes place during the mid-1500s, a grim period in Nordic history, and is set in the province of Bohuslän on the western coast of Sweden, with its barren cliffs and desolate plains. The main theme is taken from a well-known traditional story of a murdered parson in Bohuslän, a wealthy Sir Arne who is robbed by three Scotsmen posing as journeymen tanners. After the Scotsmen steal the money, they murder everyone in the house except for a young girl, Elsalill, who manages to hide during the massacre and through whose testimony they are eventually captured. Lagerlöf's nearest source for her story was *Chorographia Bahusiensis*, a description of events in Bohuslän written by a clergyman in the 1700s. Primarily a chronicle of crimes, it supplied Lagerlöf with material for several of her stories of violence and guilt.[20]

Lagerlöf habitually based her stories on anecdotes she had either read or heard. It might have been a story handed down through generations, as in the case of *The Treasure* or, as in the case of *Jerusalem*, a newspaper article that stimulated her fantasy. Often, the story germinated in her mind for years before it took its desired form. In the case of the murder of Sir Arne, Lagerlöf attempted to give the story written form as early as 1897. The resulting short narrative, called "Hämnd får man alltid" ("One Always Gets Revenge"), is included in the posthumously published *Från skilda tider.*

As the title indicates, revenge is the main theme of the story. When *The Treasure* was published in 1904, it too had revenge as an important theme, but it was balanced by the themes of love, guilt, and sacrifice. The main story line of *The Treasure* centers on the meeting after the murder between the unsuspecting Elsalill and Sir Archie, the murderer, on her awakened feelings of love for him, and on the painful decision she must make when she begins to suspect who he is. Her desire to have the new home and social position he promises her is at odds with her demand for justice. The anguish caused by conflicting interests, perhaps the most important theme in Lagerlöf's works, is brought to a head in *The Treasure*.

The narrative follows its folktale source closely. In both cases, three men, dressed as tanners in animal skins, storm into Sir Arne's house, steal his money, and murder everyone present, with only a young girl escaping the bloodbath. What Lagerlöf adds is the love interest and the moral conflict, which give her story vitality and significance. She also created a new character for *The Treasure* in the fishmonger Torarin, a figure of complex significance, as Lagerlöf's secondary characters often are. While his role is essentially that of outside observer and commentator, he also serves to further the plot. He takes the surviving young girl with him to his lowly cabin in Marstrand, where she is given hard work to do. His mother takes her to be a fish cleaner on the quays, where she meets three Scottish gentlemen, finely clad and apparently rich. One of them, Sir Archie, begins to court her and promises her a life of luxury and abundance. He asks her to come with him to Scotland, where he soon will be sailing with his two companions. Elsalill, who is unhappy with her dreary life in Marstrand, is charmed by the elegant Scotsman and tempted by his offer. But his enticing promises are opposed in Elsalill's conscience by the recollection of the crime, for her mission is to restore the order upset by Sir Archie's hideous deed. Elsalill belongs to the dead, who draw her to themselves with signs and mementos. Communication with persons on the other side of life is included in the story as something perfectly natural. Elsalill's dead foster sister is even forced to appear in the world of the living in order to see to it that revenge is carried out. As is typical in ghost stories, the dead cannot rest in their graves until their assailants have been punished. The foster sister can be understood as a materialization of Elsalill's anxiety and her unconscious suspicions concerning the three Scotsmen. Inseparable in life, the two young girls, after the death of the foster sister, fuse together into a single person whose purpose is to be an instrument of justice (as young innocent girls always are in Lagerlöf's works).

On one level, *The Treasure* is a detective story that deals with exposing and apprehending criminals. By the time Lagerlöf wrote this story, she had gained such a command of her narrative technique that she was able to attempt some highly unusual scenes. For example, she has the dead foster sister take a position as a dishwasher in a tavern in Marstrand so that she might keep an eye on the Scottish mercenaries who gather there. (A ghost who washes dishes might be without counterpart in world literature.) The messages from her foster sister make it impossible for Elsalill to deny the knowledge that the Sir Archie she loves is in fact her sister's murderer. The problem finds expression, in typical Lagerlöf fashion, in the masks the characters wear in different situations; behind Sir Archie's guise as a cavalier, for example, lurks the cruelty and rapaciousness of his true nature. Or does it? It is the margin of uncertainty in Lagerlöf's character depiction that lends an extra vital dimension to her narratives.

Sir Archie's horrible deed affects even the entire natural and social environment of the place in which the story is set. Marstrand, so dependent on navigation, lies completely hemmed in by ice. Spring refuses to come, and the ship on which the Scotsmen impatiently wait to sail home cannot put to sea. Here, as in many other instances in Lagerlöf's works, nature has taken on an anthropomorphic character, and the crime of Sir Archie and his cohorts has evoked the nemesis of nature. While this theme is prominent in works as early as *Gösta Berling's Saga,* nowhere in Lagerlöf's oeuvre is it demonstrated with such force as in *The Treasure.* To point up the heinous crime of cutting short a human life long before its time, Lagerlöf employs the analogy of a poor young birch tree that has been chopped down just as it started to sprout leaves (the same image she uses in *The Tale of a Manor*).

The Treasure takes on the characteristics of a thriller when, toward the end, all the different ways that lead to exposing and capturing the three Scotsmen are depicted. At this point, the psychological and moral problems are also brought to a head. Even after she has betrayed the man she loves, Elsalill wants to escape with him to his country and give up thoughts of revenge. But there is no future for her; it has been cut off by Sir Archie's hideous crime. The image of the tree that has been lopped off applies to Elsalill as well as to her foster sister. All her fantasies about a bright future are based on the repression of the terrible deed she witnessed when all those she loved were murdered. When Sir Archie learns that Elsalill has exposed him and unfeelingly recounts for her everything that happened on the day of the murder, she is brought back to reality—a reality that is unbearable and that kills her. After listening to Sir Archie pour out his scorn for her and boast about how the murderers had fooled those who tried to track them down, she "could scarce feel her heart beating." Her final sacrifice occurs almost mechanically. At the same moment in which Sir Archie tries to escape the pikes of the guards by holding Elsalill in front of him as a shield, she seizes one of the pikes and drives it into her heart.

Sir Archie escapes and reaches the ship that is to sail for Scotland. But the ice continues to hold the vessel in its grip; it even refuses to break up when the murderers, through the intervention of the fishmonger Torarin, are caught and taken back to Marstrand. Only when the dead Elsalill is taken from the ship do conditions return to normal. A long procession of women and young lads come out on the ice and carry her back to town. With this homage to the dead girl, the somber story fades out in the manner of a legend. The young girl is elevated to martyrdom, and nature reacts as if heaving a powerful sigh. After the women carry Elsalill away, the waves are released and surge forth to break up and clear away the ice. The ship can finally sail—without the three murderers.

The carefully maintained suspense and the dramatic conclusion make *The Treasure* such a gripping literary experience that the story has invited adaptations for other media. It has been filmed twice, the first time in 1919 by the highly acclaimed Swedish director Mauritz Stiller, who made the story into an exceptionally beautiful silent film.[21] The German dramatist Gerhart Hauptmann undertook to rework *The Treasure* into a drama in verse, *Winterballade* (1917), which Lagerlöf could not resist adapting for the Swedish stage. But her dramatization enjoyed only one performance (in 1918), and that was not a success, for although Lagerlöf was strongly attracted to the theater, she was no dramatist.[22] Several composers have also been interested in *The Treasure*. In the 1960s, it was performed as an opera, with congenial music by the Swedish composer Gösta Nystroem.

Critics and scholars hold contradictory views of *The Treasure*. Some find the work a simple ghost story with no deeper meaning. Others, such as Gunnel Weidel and Louise Winge, have delved deeply into the structure and symbolism of the work.[23] Recently a new feminist interpretation has been published in the United States, where an edition of *The Treasure,* with an introduction by Jane Arnold, was put out by the feminist publishing firm of Daughters, Inc. (1973). Arnold sees the work as "an allegory of sisterhood," since Elsalill places the interests of her sister above all else, and the men are only "interested in money, murder, and revenge." The final scene, in which the women from Marstrand carry home the dead girl, is a grandiose expression of female protest. The women "carry her back 'with all the honor that is her due.' "

A more thorough feminist reading of *The Treasure* by the American scholar Cheri Register appeared in the Swedish journal *Ord och bild* in 1979. Register bases her interpretation on Joseph Campbell's book *The Hero with a Thousand Faces* (1968) and maintains that *The Treasure* is a myth about a female sacrificial hero. Elsalill struggles against the tyrant (Sir Archie) and sacrifices her life in protest against the warlike and patriarchal system of morality that prevails in her society.[24] Even though this interpretation is one-sided, it points up an important facet of Lagerlöf's perception of women. The young, emotional girl is a more active character and one with greater power than she previously was thought to be.

Chapter Six
Novels of the 1910s

In the ten years between 1910 and 1920, Lagerlöf wrote four novels—
*Liljecronas hem (Liliecrona's Home), Körkarlen (Thy Soul Shall Bear
Witness), Kejsarn av Portugallien (The Emperor of Portugallia),* and
Bannlyst (The Outcast). She also published the first part of a two-
volume collection of short stories, *Troll och människor (Trolls and
Men,* 1915).

The work from this decade is many-faceted, with the stories
treating various subjects and set in different locales. It has been
asserted that Lagerlöf was attempting during this period to adapt
to more modern ways of thinking than she previously had embraced
by dealing with difficult contemporary social problems in her fiction.[1] It could be argued, however, that from the very beginning
of her career, her works reveal an involvement in social matters, as
they take up the existential questions involving life, death, and
moral values. In this respect, the works of the 1910s do not differ.
This does not mean that Lagerlöf's world view is static; on the
contrary, she is a human being who is constantly seeking and striving, a writer for whom the struggle for harmony becomes increasingly absorbing and complicated. In the new works, she delves
deeper into complex psychological problems, such as mental illness,
maliciousness, and pathological jealousy, than she did earlier. These
novels deal mostly with how human beings plague and torment one
another. Also, the experience of expulsion and contempt, which she
had always treated, dominates the novels of the 1910s. The characters are deprived of their homes and of love and must struggle
hard to attain their real identity.

At the same time, the plots of these novels are arranged, as they
are in earlier works, according to an optimistic plan in which love
and reconciliation win out in the end. There is without a doubt a
certain discrepancy between the underlying anguish in the works
and the calm, logical composition in which the elements of the plot
are arranged into a harmonious and meaningful order. Despite the
fact that they reveal a pessimistic insight into the consuming powers

of destruction and self-destruction, these books conclude, almost irrationally, by illustrating the conquering power of love. They deal primarily with how a person is freed from the chains that bind him to his guilt. The theme of imprisonment and release coincides, on the whole, with that of guilt and reconciliation. These basic themes are found, with a wealth of variations, in the novels of the 1910s, in which Lagerlöf achieves in places a more powerful realism than she does in her earlier works. Also in these novels, she depicts a deeper anguish and creates a symbolic language more inclined to burst the boundaries between the real and the transcendent than she ever did before in her fiction. The Värmland stories *Liliecrona's Home* and *The Emperor of Portugallia* have the additional quality of a marked naive stance. These works are, in a sense, links in the chain of development that leads to the more direct autobiographical works in the Mårbacka series.

Liliecrona's Home

Liliecrona's Home (1911) is a novel about a family, set in the days of Lagerlöf's grandmother, when Mårbacka, called Lövdala in the novel, was a rectory. As the title indicates, the narrative centers on the home itself. The description of interiors, objects, and household activities are not only very important for the novel, they also give evidence of Lagerlöf's interest in practical matters, which was awakened when she installed herself in her ancestral home. The book can be regarded as the beginning of Lagerlöf's memoirs, even though she uses the symbolic language of the fairy tale, as well as fictitious names of places and characters. This stylistic method enables her to discuss openly the difficult problems and the destructive actions that can cause an apparently peaceful home to come apart at the seams— the tensions she did not allow to surface in the Mårbacka books.

Liliecrona's Home covers the entire scale from realism to myth with a boldness scarcely present in any of Lagerlöf's works since *Gösta Berling's Saga*. The psychological aspects of the novel grow out of an unusually daring interplay containing mystifying elements. Maja Lisa, the young daughter at the rectory (for whom Lagerlöf's grandmother was the model) is cast in the role of Snow White, the tormented stepdaughter. She is also, however, an ordinary motherless girl who loves her father, hates her stepmother, and waits for her rescuer, who never seems to come. Raklitz, the stepmother, is the most genuinely mystical character in the novel. She is actually a troll, an undine who has been changed into a human by marrying a human being, the pastor at Lövdala. In everyday life, she appears as a clever and capable housewife; she is, however, markedly materialistic and does not shy away from any means to pursue her own ends. Finally, like Märta Dohna in *Gösta Berling's Saga,* she becomes a victim of her own destructiveness; when her wickedness is fully revealed, she disappears without a trace, changed once again into an undine.

The pastor, who commits the fateful mistake of marrying an evil woman, belongs more completely in the realm of reality. The novel describes the destructive process, both psychic and physical, that he undergoes. It is possible that Lagerlöf, through the character of the pastor, is depicting the fate of her own father.

The work is primarily a novel about love's struggle against imprisonment and death. Maja Lisa is, in the end, liberated from the iron cage of her home by the young violinist Liliecrona. She in turn releases him from his consuming feelings of guilt, which can be traced back to the demon of music.

When Lagerlöf wrote *Liliecrona's Home,* she had experienced both being forced to leave and being able to return to her home and the security it offered. In the depiction of Maja Lisa's path to freedom, which in a lyrical way summarizes her grandmother's story, one perceives the image of Lagerlöf herself, who at one time wandered the paths around "Lövdala" and dreamed of becoming a writer. Upon her return to Värmland, she might have experienced a spiritual confrontation with herself as a young girl. The threat of losing her ancestral home became a theme of anxiety in *Liliecrona's Home,* as it is in so many of Lagerlöf's works. While the roots and the traditions of Mårbacka may have become a source of inspiration for her writing in the coming decades, however, Lagerlöf also left Mårbacka often to seek out other localities and experiences to write about.

Thy Soul Shall Bear Witness

In *Thy Soul Shall Bear Witness* (1912), Lagerlöf enters the boundary land between life and death. This short novel is, to a certain extent, a commissioned work. The National Tuberculosis Society had asked Lagerlöf to help educate the public about tuberculosis. In *The Won-*

derful Adventures of Nils, she had taken up the subject. She herself had experienced the illness at close hand when her sister Anna died of it as a young woman.

Lagerlöf first became seriously involved in social matters during her years in Landskrona, and it was that city that came to mind when she chose the setting for *Thy Soul Shall Bear Witness.* In the book, however, the locale does not have a name nor is a precise year for the action given, but it can be assumed that the story takes place during the period of modern industrialization, since its main character, David Holm, is a factory worker. More important is the actual time span of the action, which is concentrated in the hours around the stroke of midnight on a New Year's Eve. In an exaggerated manner, as in a dream, everything happens very fast, but is somehow drawn out as if minutes were years. While Lagerlöf places the stress on tuberculosis by having several of her main characters suffer from the disease, she subordinates the practical discussion of the illness to questions of guilt and atonement—always basic in Lagerlöf's works.

Lagerlöf herself has mentioned that Dickens's *A Christmas Carol* was a model for her story, in which her main character, like Ebenezer Scrooge, is confronted by his past. The myth of the ferryman of death, on which her narrative is based, comes from a fairy tale of Brittany, set down by Anatole Le Braz.[2] According to the tale, the last person who dies in the old year is given the task of returning as a spirit to pick up the dying and transport them in a cart into the realm of death until he is relieved of his duties by a new coachman on the following New Year's Eve.

The man in the story intended to play the role of death's driver on New Year's Eve is David Holm, a rowdy character and alcoholic who suffers from tuberculosis. David's *fylgja* ("guardian angel") is Edith, a young Salvation Army slum worker, who loves him and sets his salvation as her goal. When she learns that he is married, she suppresses her disappointment and determines to help his family.

David is one of the more destructive of Lagerlöf's protagonists; he deliberately drags his wife and children with him to ruin and sadistically exposes Edith to scorn and contempt. He even becomes the cause of Edith's death, since she contracts tuberculosis when she tries to mend his coat, which is impregnated with tubercle bacilli.

The juxtaposition of a pure woman and a sin-laden man has been popular in literature at least since the romantic period, and it is present in several of Lagerlöf's works—in the contrasting pairs of Gösta Berling and Ebba Dohna, Sir Archie and Elsalill, and Edward Rhånge and Sigrun in *The Outcast*. In their relationships, love is closely connected with death, an affinity that lends a special, morbid dream atmosphere to the erotic motif. In *Thy Soul Shall Bear Witness*, the relationship between the main characters develops, as it were, as a game involving death.

When the story begins, both the male and female protagonists are near death. Edith is lying in her bed, being cared for by people who love her. David Holm, on the other hand, is lying unconscious in the grounds of the city church, hated by most and loved only by Edith, whose last wish is to be able to meet him and enable him somehow to lead a better life. She is plagued by guilt feelings because she wrongly interfered in his family affairs, thereby only worsening the situation of his wife and children. Edith begs her friends in the Salvation Army to bring David to her deathbed. But all is in vain. Scoffing, David refuses to go to her. Instead, he picks a fight with some of Edith's friends, falls down covered with blood, and remains lying where he fell.

The messenger of death arrives in the symbolic form of the coachman with a cart, which, creaking loudly, approaches David just as the church bells above him have "tolled out twelve resounding peals." The coachman of the shabby carriage, with its limping horse, is Georges, the man largely responsible for David's downfall. Georges despairs over having to turn over the gruesome task to his former friend, whose ruin he himself has brought about. He attempts, however, with carefully chosen words, to get David to accept his situation; still, he encounters nothing but David's terrible anger. At this, Georges is changed into the implacable character of death, and he binds David with ropes and casts him up onto his cart. This entire scene, which alternates between dream and reality, exhibits Lagerlöf's mastery of the genre of the ghost story. It is not surprising that *Thy Soul Shall Bear Witness* has attracted filmmakers, who have exploited all the visual and acoustical effects that the mood of the story offers.[3]

As the story continues, David is confronted by his past in three different scenes in which people are preparing to die; sets of three are always important in Lagerlöf's narrative technique. First David is led to Edith's deathbed. Unseen, he listens to her speak. Although what he hears is a recapitulation of his wicked acts, he nevertheless

becomes aware of the extent of Edith's love for him. Seized by
rapture and with great suffering, he manages to approach her bed.
She notices his presence as a shadow, and she is able to die happy
when the coachman speaks the words: "You captive, you loved one,
come out of your prison!"

After this, David returns to the miserable equipage to be taken
to the next station, a prison. He is forced to learn the bitter truth
that his brother, whom he had once loved and respected highly, is
a prisoner dying of tuberculosis and that he himself is responsible
for his brother's misfortune. He becomes steeped in guilt and in-
trospection. The journey back becomes a kind of purgatory. David's
path to atonement and reconciliation is illustrated not only concretely but symbolically as well, when the ropes with which he is
bound are gradually loosened. At the same time, on the concrete
level there appears a possibility for atonement. David promises to
fulfill his brother's last wish—to help a crippled boy who has become
his friend. The child needs to go to a spa and take salt baths (this
part of the story reflects Lagerlöf's own childhood problem, as described in *Mårbacka*).

The third, and decisive, scene presents a confrontation between
David Holm and his wife. He is taken to her miserable slum dwell-
ing, where there is hardly a piece of furniture left. Unseen, he and
the coachman witness the preparations being made by his wife for
killing her children and taking her own life. David, begging the
coachman to save her, is prepared to make the greatest sacrifice—
to leave the world and live in eternal darkness—if only his wife
and children can remain alive. With this offer, his inner change is
complete. Georges, who also has sins to atone for, takes upon himself
the coachman's duties for one more year, thus freeing David from
this dreadful task in the land of the dead. This also means that
David must leave the world of the spirits and return once again·to
the duress of earthly life. The coachman's antiformula, "You captive,
return to your prison," allows David to once again receive a living
human body.

At this point, the story returns to the garden of the church, where
David is lying. He gets up and on tottering legs stumbles home to
his wife. She is horrified when she sees him again, but she becomes
convinced of his good intentions when he breaks into tears of despair
(tears are often of great emotional significance in Lagerlöf's works).
While David now longs for his final liberation when he will meet

Edith again, he realizes that he must devote himself to life on earth, with its duties and responsibilities. Those are the conditions that will enable his soul to mature before it can be harvested. Lagerlöf's message is more clearly expressed here than it is in most of her books. Indeed, she even pointed out in a letter that in *Thy Soul Shall Bear Witness* she deviated from her usual practice of not sermonizing. But she hoped that this novel would be a book that would appeal to a wide public.[4]

In *Thy Soul Shall Bear Witness,* Lagerlöf dissolved the boundary line between reality and transcendence. As is often the case in such a narrative, various possibilities for interpreting the text arise. One can read the work as a realistic narrative about a man who is asleep, awakens from his horrible dreams, and influenced by these dreams, attempts to start life anew. On another plane, the book is a conventional ghost story about a man who ends up in the realm of death, but is allowed to return to life. The narrative develops into an ideological description of the struggle between the spiritual and the material. Edith represents pure spiritual power, expressed in unselfish love. Her mission is to bring out the soul of this "wild man" which, though deeply hidden, does indeed exist. This idea is not unknown in world literature; Beatrice and Dante, Gretchen and Faust, and Solveig and Peer Gynt are couples who illustrate how feminine goodness and spirituality rescue man from damnation.

The dream of liberation from earthly troubles, from the shackles of life, is one of the essential aspects of Lagerlöf's psychological makeup. In no other book has she created this dream as vividly as in *Thy Soul Shall Bear Witness.* In this work, she goes deeper into the existence on the other side of life than she does in any previous work. At the same time, the book is a story about social misery, occasionally with an almost brutal objectivity. It appears to combine irreconcilable elements; a realistic depiction of slums and physical decay is united with an ecstatic vision of purity and infinite mercy. As Alrik Gustafson sums it up, "The art of this tale resembles expressionism in its strange blending of realism and fantasy, its stark, terrifying visionary quality."[5]

The basic theme of *Thy Soul Shall Bear Witness,* which has variations on a number of levels, is that of captivity and liberation. It is expressed most clearly in the formula with which the coachman calls people from life to freedom in the realm of the spirits: "You captive, break out of your prison." The notion of the body as a

prison for the soul goes back as far as Plato. The tendency to regard
life on earth as imprisonment became fundamental for the romantics,
and it reappeared, to a certain extent, in the literature of the 1890s.
Disgust with the material world and the longing to be free from
the chains of existence were thoughts that especially saturated the
spiritualistic and theosophical doctrines that were considerable, and
influential, in Sweden around the turn of the century. Without
becoming affiliated with any orthodox movement, Lagerlöf was already interested in theosophical studies at the same time that she
was writing *Gösta Berling's Saga*. "I believe that heaven is open but
that we are imprisoned," is the revealing statement she made in a
letter of 1886.[6] The theme of the imprisoned human being striving
for freedom does not appear in as pure a form in any of her works
as it does in *Thy Soul Shall Bear Witness*.

Lagerlöf did not write her book in order to make propaganda for
any theosophical doctrine. It certainly seems, however, that her
interest in theosophy was given new impetus in the 1910s, when
she apparently received support for one of her favorite ideas, that
man possesses hidden powers which can be awakened and used to
achieve positive ends.[7]

In order to extend her view of life and her sense of values, Lagerlöf
in *Thy Soul Shall Bear Witness*, sought the realm of death. In her
next book, she wanders back to Värmland, but there too she concerns
herself with the outlying regions of the soul, in order to investigate
life's basic questions as clearly and as dramatically as possible.

The Emperor of Portugallia

Of the four novels that Lagerlöf wrote during the 1910s, *The
Emperor of Portugallia* (1914) is the most important artistically, as
well as the most humanly gripping. Once again she returns to the
provincial life around Lake Löven, but not to the sparkling life of
the manors that she portrayed in *Gösta Berling's Saga*. Instead, she
centers this novel on the life of the poor tenant farmers on the edge
of the forest. The narrative method and style are also changed;
Lagerlöf uses a good deal of dialect, and she presents her story in
an intimate and empathetic manner. The main character is Jan of
Ruffluck Croft (Jan i Skrolycka), a day laborer whose love for his
daughter is so great that he slips into a deep psychosis when she
leaves home, illustrating the theme of mental illness as a refuge
from an unbearable reality.

While the novel deals with anxiety and fear, the main theme, perhaps, as Kjell Wallström has suggested, is the idea of the re-creating power of love, its almost metaphysical power, expressed first and foremost in the classical tragic motif of all-consuming fatherly love.[8] Lagerlöf once suggested to her publisher that the book should be called *A Swedish King Lear*.[9] Balzac's well-known novel *Le Père Goriot* should also be mentioned in this connection. In both cases, the father does not fail the adult daughters, even though they have grown hard and unmerciful.

The first chapter of the novel shows how the poor tenant is overcome by emotions he has never before known. It is as if he were reborn on the day he becomes a father. Jan's love for his daughter, which gives rise to his love for humanity, provides him with an almost supernatural ability to interpret signs and omens and to make predictions; on the popular, naive level dominant in the narration, his deeds take on the nature of miracles. The subsequent story illustrates in short anecdotes the love between father and daughter. The Biblical allusions appear to be almost innumerable in *The Emperor of Portugallia,* with the poor family in the crofter's cottage taking on an aura of the Holy Family,[10] and, to a certain extent, the novel develops along the lines of the legend.

But the book is not a Christian allegory; it has many levels of meaning. Contrasting with the Biblical elements are the disquieting elements related to nature, the forest, the sun, and the color red. Jan declares that the sun will be his little girl's godmother, and, accordingly, he names her Glory Goldie Sunnycastle (Klara Fina Gulleborg). A red dress made of material given her by a traveling salesman when she is fifteen years old becomes a symbol of breaking away, for it leads to Glory Goldie's wanting to leave home. The day she shows off her red dress in church for all the parish to see is the acme of joy and triumph for her whole family. It is also a day of hubris, however, to be followed by a time of suffering, which begins when the new, hard-hearted master of the manor, Lars Gunnarsson, threatens to take Jan and Katrina's humble cottage from them. Here appears the recognizable theme of the threatened home, so frequent in Lagerlöf's works. The girl offers to go to Stockholm to earn the money necessary to pay off Lars Gunnarsson, and she is able to send the money by the day it is due. But she herself does not return.

Jan's despair over his daughter's disappearance goes through different stages. When he hears the rumor that she has become a prostitute in Stockholm, his mental illness takes the form of megalomania. He announces to all those around him that he is an emperor and that his daughter, whose return he constantly awaits, is an empress. In his fantasy, he adorns her with gold and beautiful clothes. His description of her "with a crown of gold upon her head, and with seven kings behind her holding up her royal mantle, and seven tame lions crouched at her feet" shows clearly an influence of the description of the Biblical Babylonian whore. The empress becomes her father's guiding star, and he interprets everything that happens as a sign from her. He thereby creates the relationship with his daughter which had been his sole reason for living.

Jan's ridiculous appearance—he decks himself out with gold stars and other emblems—awakens different reactions from the people around him. The wicked and primitive ones show him scorn and contempt, while the good and faithful ones exhibit sympathy and concern. The story is, among other things, a sharp-sighted study of social consciousness in connection with a demented person. Lagerlöf proves herself a master of psychological insight with her depiction of the relationship of Jan and his work-worn wife Katrina. In her matter-of-fact, realistic way, Katrina realizes that her husband is "crazy," but she supports him through thick and thin. He in turn has a positive influence on her; she develops into a convincing and absorbing character, a forerunner of many poor, heroic women in later Swedish popular literature.

Their unhappy situation brings Jan and Katrina together, causing them to develop new spiritual qualities. It is Katrina who above all points out that Jan is more than a mere demented creature; he is a person with strong moral feelings, a man whose unusual sensitivity gives him a strange power over people and events. Lagerlöf has been praised for her ability to describe in accurate detail the emperor's psychosis. On the whole, her characterization is clinically unassailable. But it is not primarily a case of mental illness that she wanted to write about. Going beyond the normal was for her a means of cultivating feelings and attitudes. Like a Don Quixote, the emperor provides the basic human experiences of suffering and compassion and of joy and dignity. Jan also becomes something of a poet, with a strong sensitivity for everything that upsets the balance in his own existence and in the lives of those around him.

In Lagerlöf's works, the most serious disturbance in the moral system is represented by the generation gap. For her, to sin against one's parents meant cutting off the most essential relationship of one's existence—a relationship that must be re-established. That is why, for example, the sin of the Major's Wife against her mother is so important in *Gösta Berling's Saga*. In other works, too, the conflict between generations is very significant. In *The Miracles of Antichrist,* the sin of the daughter against her father is a central theme, and both *Charlotte Löwensköld* and *Anna Svärd* are based on the theme of the mother-son conflict. But in no other work is the motif of the fourth commandment as dominant as in *The Emperor of Portugallia,* in which the main problem is the daughter's desertion of her father. The theme is strengthened by a series of parallel situations.

A long, central chapter of the novel has the nature of a partitura for the fourth commandment, which bids children to honor their father and mother. In three carefully executed variations on the theme, Lagerlöf takes up the question of the relationships between grown children and their parents. In all three situations, in which old people are threatened by the hard-heartedness of their adult children, Jan steps in to help solve the conflict. Through him, Lars Gunnarsson is punished for having failed his father-in-law and mother-in-law. Jan can, in a sense, be seen as an instrument of nemesis. But on the other hand he also helps people to attain happiness and saves their relationships. These secondary themes serve as a background for and as illustrations of the major theme, the relationship between Glory Goldie and her father. The solution of that conflict forms the dramatic conclusion of the novel.

As is often the case in Lagerlöf's works, the path to reconciliation involves a difficult restoration of the original, genuine personality. This is the path that the Major's Wife had to take in *Gösta Berling's Saga,* and it must also be taken by the daughter in *The Emperor of Portugallia.* But first the break between the generations is made complete. When after an absence of fifteen years Glory Goldie shows up in her childhood home, ugly and coarse, she is seized by an aversion to her father, that crazy man who appears as a parody of Napoleon. She decides to leave home in secrecy and to take her mother with her.

But she does not succeed in severing the strong ties that bind her to her father. Just as the boat with Glory Goldie and the

remorseful Katrina leaves the pier, Jan comes running and throws
himself into the water. He drowns immediately, and his body cannot
be found.

Now a new stage in the relationship between father and daughter
begins. Day in and day out the daughter wanders about the pier,
anxiously waiting for her father's body to be found. She has had a
coffin built for him, which also stands on the pier, ready to receive
his body. Her efforts are made not out of love but out of fear. In
her imagination, her father has been changed to a real emperor,
"powerful and awe-inspiring," a kind of sea king who sits at the
bottom of the lake, demanding her life. She feels a strange temptation to lay herself down in the coffin and glide out onto the lake,
to sink down to her judge.

The story is brought to its point of reconciliation, however, when
Glory Goldie learns, finally, that her father did not try to punish
her with his death but, on the contrary, had cast himself into the
water in order to save her. Her mother, who died of grief, confirms
on her deathbed the good will of her husband.

The last chapter develops into a grandiose collective scene, with
one of the processions that Lagerlöf loves so well. After Jan's body
is found, both Katrina and Jan are given a stately funeral, with the
whole parish marching in the procession—befitting an "emperor."
It is not an emperor they are paying homage to, however, but the
tenant farmer with the warmest heart in the district. The creative
power of her father's love now touches Glory Goldie. She feels
suddenly that she is living in "a world filled with love," in which
she re-experiences her childhood days with her father. The relationship is restored, and the reconciliation is complete. In Lagerlöf's
customary manner, the conciliatory event is also reflected in the
character's physical appearance. Once again, Glory Goldie becomes
young and beautiful, as did the Major's Wife on her deathbed; thus
for Lagerlöf, the moral solution is also an aesthetic one.

The Emperor of Portugallia came out during the same year that
World War I began. It can be assumed that the action of the novel
takes place at some time during the 1870s, since Lagerlöf includes
herself and her sister in their childhood years, "the little misses of
Lövdala," as supernumeraries in the narrative. The depiction of life
in the secluded province appears to have no connection with the
catastrophic world situation. But the question arises whether the

extremely hot, anxiety-ridden summer of 1914 did not contribute to the story's heightened atmosphere of confusion and fear.

Perhaps *The Emperor of Portugallia* should be regarded as Lagerlöf's most important message of the day, the message of love that passes all understanding, written against a background of fear.

Selma Lagerlöf's Pacifism

Throughout her life, the idea of peace was foremost in Lagerlöf's mind. In her opinion, war belonged to a primitive stage in the development of mankind, a stage that had to be overcome and surpassed. Even though she undoubtedly exhibited a certain fascination for wild and destructive attitudes, from early on she took an uncompromising stand against war. In several instances, she described the fear of, and the terrible effects of, war. Actual depictions of war scenes are scarcely to be found in her works, though, perhaps because she was a writer in a country that had fortunately escaped the experiences of war during her entire lifetime.

Lagerlöf's involvement with peace movements began during the 1880s, when she became strongly engaged in various progressive movements of the time; this involvement is reflected in *Gösta Berling's Saga*. At the end of the novel, she introduces an old soldier, Jan Hök, as a mouthpiece for her pacifism. Jan Hök feels that he has been stained by his participation in war: "everyone hated him, because he had spilled blood and caused injury." The real person behind this fictive character is found in *Mårbacka*. As a child, Lagerlöf once had to visit an old soldier who lived in a cottage deep in the forest. She was told that under no circumstances should she talk with him about war, because he would be frightfully upset. But she became scared at the idea of meeting a person who would not want to converse with her about his terrible experiences. Through literature, she had already been indoctrinated to believe that a warrior was a hero.

The collection *Invisible Links* contains several antiwar stories. "Romarblod" ("Roman Blood"), which originated in connection with Lagerlöf's journey to Italy in the 1890s, depicts how a "true Roman woman" reacts to Italy's colonial war in Abysinnia. The story has a paradoxical development. Young women in Italy are expected, according to proud traditions, to honor their men when they go to war. But Teresa in "Roman Blood" wounds her fiancé with a knife in order to keep him from being sent to the front. [11] Another woman who sacrifices everything for peace is Margareta Fredkulla in *The Queens of Kungahälla,* who actually marries for peace when she becomes the bride of a war lord she does not know. This story, which describes the devastating effects of war in a border village, is also based on a paradox. It is an example of how the masculine and feminine opposites correspond, as a rule, with the contrast between war and peace. In Lagerlöf's fictive world, the masculine is closely related to the martial, while the feminine is related to the home, children, and patient work. The "heroes" who destroy the accomplishments of the Major's Wife in *Gösta Berling's Saga* have, in general, a military past, and the imagery used in connection with these characters is sometimes colored by military expressions.

A darker atmosphere dominates *The Treasure,* in which the masculine, warlike world contrasts sharply with the feminine sphere it threatens. *Christ Legends,* however, offers the strongest contrast between soldiers and those who cannot defend themselves. "Betlehems barn" ("The Children of Bethlehem"), the story of Herod's slaughter of the innocents, contains a ghastly scene in which the mothers of the children confront a horde of hardened, robot-like soldiers, instruments of the high powers. Another story in the same collection depicts how the wife of the Roman procurator Pontius Pilate rises up in rebellion for the sake of peace. Here, militarism is opposed by the peaceful message of the Bible. The wounded and those grieving for their loved ones lost on the battlefield cry out in unison for Jesus, who "will reshape the spears into lyres and the swords into vineyard knives."

The difference between the masculine, warlike activities and the feminine desire for preservation can be seen clearly in the famous speech that Lagerlöf delivered at the World Congress of Women in 1911, "Home and State," published in *Trolls and Men.* The speech is a vehement attack on the masculine attitude: men have built great nations, based on violence and destruction. The creation of women, the home, is the center of edifying powers, providing a social safety net and the breeding ground for cultural activities. This idea points to later discussions about women's own culture and special opportunities for women to work for peace.

A few years after Lagerlöf criticized militarism in "Home and State," World War I broke out; she now began receiving requests from near and far to use her pen in the service of peace. [12]

The pressure to relate everything she wrote to the current war was too much for her; so many demands had a paralyzing effect, and she experienced a productivity crisis. She did, nevertheless, attempt to experiment with certain new forms and symbols, as evidenced by "Sex stämningar från krigsåren" ("Six Pictures from the War Years"), published in 1921 in the second part of *Trolls and Men*. These stories are also an allegorical expression of her agony in the face of something she could neither really understand nor mitigate. She lived in her idyll at Mårbacka, enclosed by a garden. The cries of those who suffered did, nevertheless, penetrate into her peaceful existence, cutting into her security and destroying her desire to create. In "The Ravaged Church," she gives vent to her sorrow over her inability to write because her soul is "full of images of fear and terror." It is "mute, without bells, without song."

The Outcast

Gradually, the inspiration to write began to return and Lagerlöf started work on *Bannlyst* (*The Outcast,* 1918) a novel containing her pacifist creed. It was based on the idea that war is as repugnant and loathsome as cannibalism and therefore unjustifiable for civilized human beings. This thought provides the basis for the novel's all-too-ingenious design; Lagerlöf combines an ideological story that treats war allegorically with a story of marriage, actually a novel in itself. Although their plots are intertwined and are intended to symbolically illuminate one another, there is a distinct gap between the marital story and the peace novel.

The first part of *The Outcast,* set in Bohuslän on Sweden's west coast, shows the renewed force of Lagerlöf's imagination after her period of nonproductivity. Never before has she described the sea in such a manner. She is able to capture, lyrically and with precision, the cliffs and the water, the variations of light and shadows, and the infinite feeling of freedom that the sea imparts. Her description of the sea also provides the symbolic background for the main female character, Sigrun, whose mystic relationship with the sea is reminiscent of Ibsen's *The Lady from the Sea.* Like Ibsen's Ellida, Sigrun is a foreigner in the district where she lives. She feels confined and stifled, both by the dismal countryside and by her marriage, in which her husband Edvard Rhånge, pastor of the district, keeps jealous watch over her. When she meets Sven Elversson, who shows

her the sea, a dramatic triangle of a very special nature develops.
Then a fourth character is added, Sigrun's childhood friend Lotta
Hedman, who has a peculiar role of seer. As usual in Lagerlöf's
novels, the main characters are backed up by a series of secondary
figures; the most clearly drawn of these are Sven Elversson's parents.

The four central characters, whose fates are woven together, have
in common the fact that they all suffer from antagonistic relationships with those around them, living lives of misery, disgrace, and
humility until the final redress. While they all are outcasts of one
kind or another, Sven Elversson is ostracized in a more official sense.
Elversson, who comes from a poor fisherman's family, was adopted
as a child by a rich English family, who raised him and provided
for his education. He becomes a promising scientist and participates
in a bold polar expedition. This marks the beginning of the tragic
action that changes his success to misfortune. The members of the
expedition, honored upon their return home, soon fall into disgrace
when the rumor arises that they had eaten human flesh during
periods of starvation on the polar ice. Sven, who was so weak and
dazed during the expedition that he has no recollection of the situation, is unable to defend himself.

When his English family rejects him, he finds his way back to
his biological parents, who receive him as a lost son. In the rest of
the district, however, he is an outcast. Edvard Rhånge comments
on Sven's actions in a sermon in which he vents his utter disgust
and which has the effect of an official banishment. Throughout the
rest of the novel, Elversson must struggle in vain against the disgust
of the people, symbolized by a powerful, lurking cat.

In Lagerlöf's works, banishment is most often connected with
guilt. The story line usually reflects a moral development, with the
banished one fighting to regain the respect and honor so important
for Lagerlöf's protagonists. When the protagonist is established in
the moral order, he is also accepted by society in general. This is
essentially what happens in *The Outcast,* the difference being that
in this book, the one who suffers from being ostracized is innocent.
He is the victim of rumors and prejudices. In a sense, he becomes
a Christ figure. [13]

In a series of episodes, Lagerlöf establishes Sven Elversson as a
refined character (this does not exclude physical strength) in contrast
to the harshness of those around him. With his humility and love
of mankind, he is reminiscent of Prince Myshkin in Dostoevsky's

The Idiot. He is also a new kind of male protagonist, an antihero, a hater of violence. All his actions are directed to helping the weak souls of society, yet he is regarded as "worse than the worst."

There is one person, however, who takes pity on him—Sigrun, one of Lagerlöf's good, sensitive young women. Sigrun is a new type of heroine for Lagerlöf, modeled after the English Pre-Raphaelite images of women. She is described explicitly as a higher being, whose dream is to be able to perform charitable acts of mercy in the service of mankind. But she is trapped in her home, strictly guarded by her pathologically jealous husband. Rhånge, in contrast to Elversson, often appears wild and uncontrolled; his violence within the walls of his own home exemplifies the destructiveness illustrated on another level by the war.

Sigrun's fate is essentially related to Elversson's; she too is an outcast, deprived of the opportunity to make a contribution to society. The depiction of how she finally escapes from her home after she has deceived her husband into believing that she is dead is a device that smacks of the Gothic novel, even if it has a basis in contemporary reality. Sigrun's goal is to sail to America and from there serve in the war as a nurse. Instead, her life now becomes linked to Elversson's. On her flight from home, she takes refuge in the hotel for tramps and wayfarers that Elversson established after all his attempts to be accepted in the fishing village failed.

As in several other instances in Lagerlöf's works, the lovers meet in a situation reminiscent of death. When Sigrun escapes from her husband, she willingly cuts herself off from life. Elversson too has withdrawn from actual life and exists in a state of patient submissiveness. When Sigrun comes to him, though, he takes her worries upon himself and enables her to communicate with her husband.

With this, the book is ready for the final action that will solve both the marital conflict and the ideological problem. Now Elversson assumes a more clearly defined role of savior. Through his efforts, the pattern of violence in Edvard Rhånge is broken; Rhånge gives up Sigrun and overcomes his jealousy. When the parson, in the decisive moment, masters his desire to kill his rival, he releases himself from the dreadful family curse that has been his burden. All the men in his family have plagued their wives and ended as suicides—an unavoidable consequence of a serious crime of their ancestors. This masculine destructiveness, which destroyed the lives of women and ended in self-destruction, is a manifestation of the same martial cruelty for which Lagerlöf, in *The Outcast,* sought to awaken disgust.

Sven Elversson is also liberated in the end. He unloads his burden of guilt when he takes upon himself the macabre task of burying the dead bodies the fishermen catch in their nets after the Battle of Jutland, in which thousands of men were killed at sea. These bodies, incidentally, were the "catches" that Lagerlöf herself saw when she visited Bohuslän during the war. [14] For didactic purposes, Lagerlöf juxtaposes the story line of her individual character with the larger subject of the war; her intention is that the reader should regard the crime of the outcast as insignificant, compared to the consequences of war.

Lagerlöf was not satisified with merely implying the comparison. She completely exonerated the outcast. In a letter discovered on the body of an Englishman killed in the sea battle—a man who, with Elversson, had been a member of the fateful polar expedition—proof is found that Elversson had never indulged in cannibalism. The letter clearly states that he refused to eat even one small piece of human flesh. This is not the first time that Lagerlöf has used letters to unravel the knots of a difficult and complicated intrigue, but in this case the effect of the message by letter is more far-fetched than usual. Properly speaking, however, Lagerlöf follows the same narrative technique as in her earlier works—a technique that demands that all loose ends should be gathered up and all complications should be resolved as in a well-laid game of solitaire.

Lagerlöf also includes in her plan that Rhånge, the man who at one time proclaimed Elversson's banishment, announces to the people the news of his innocence. This announcement takes place in connection with the burial of those who died in the sea battle. Rhånge's sermon takes the form of a paradoxical homage to life and to Elversson, who more than anyone else fostered the "sacredness of life." The speech is also intended to awaken disgust and repugnance toward war by means of a naturalistic description of the dead and decaying victims. Lagerlöf's readers are accustomed to finding her message implicit in the plots of her stories, but in *The Outcast* the message is expressed, less successfully, in an oration. Actually, there are two orations, for after Rhånge's didactic contribution follows, as a coda, an ecstatic attack on war and a lyrical-Biblical vision of the millennium of peace, spoken by Lotta Hedman, who now has also come to be accepted as a prophetess to whom the people are willing to listen. The differences between Sigrun and her husband must, of course, also be reconciled. Lagerlöf resolves the situation in an exceedingly simple manner, by having Elversson suffer a heart attack at the very moment of happiness, when Rhånge proclaims his innocence. He sinks to the ground during the sermon. This stroke of fate prevents the lovers from becoming entrapped in an adulterous situation. Sigrun becomes Elversson's nurse from that moment until he dies, at which time she returns to her husband, and the final reconciliation takes place.

The Outcast is essentially a grandiose failure. Its complex themes and ideas are never integrated in Lagerlöf's customary manner. The overabundance of themes also gives rise to too many melodramatic and mechanical devices. Lagerlöf herself was aware of the book's shortcomings, but she nevertheless believed that the artistic aims of the work had to be subordinated to the message; indeed, she wanted in this work to sermonize and give expression to her pathos. [15]

After dealing with the major problems of the world, especially the question of peace, like many other Swedish writers, Lagerlöf began to concern herself with "the little world"—a concern reflected in the somewhat idyllic story of her childhood, *Mårbacka* (1922). The Mårbacka series was followed by her very last novels, those comprising the trilogy on the Löwensköld family—novels that became, in many respects, the crowning synthesis of her literary production.

Chapter Seven
The Löwensköld Trilogy

The General's Ring: A Ghost Story

In the 1920s, Lagerlöf began work on a new novel *Löwensköldska ringen (The General's Ring)* which developed into the Löwensköld trilogy, a family history that spans the period from around 1700 to the 1830s. The first part, *The General's Ring* (1925) is a tale of crime, punishment, and revenge. Like *The Treasure,* with which it is often compared, it is something of a thrilling ghost story, but both in origin and design, it is rather more folkloristic than the earlier work. In the case of *The General's Ring,* Lagerlöf collected the best ghost stories from her Mårbacka childhood and used these simple tales as a basis for her novel.

The theme of grave desecration provides the basis of the novel. It begins by telling how, in 1741, a golden ring—a gift from the legendary King Charles XII—is stolen from the finger of the dead general Bengt Löwensköld of the aristocratic Löwensköld family, several months after his burial. In the epic, a ring is often an object possessing magical powers. The motif of the king's ring is also integral to what was probably Lagerlöf's most immediate source of inspiration for *The General's Ring, Fältskärns berättelser (Tales of an Army Surgeon),* the monumental work of the Finnish-Swedish writer Zacharias Topelius, which she read with enthusiasm as a thirteen-year-old at Mårbacka.[1] In 1920, she had published a monograph on Topelius for the Swedish Academy, in which she placed special emphasis on these tales of Swedish history, with their theme of a ring and the devastating power it exerts on those who wear it.

The action in *The General's Ring* is based on popular superstitions—fatalistic notions about the revenge of the dead and the idea of sins always being found out and punished. According to popular belief, if a dead person is robbed of something valuable, his ghost will return as a haunting spirit, seeking retribution for that which he has lost. As usual, Lagerlöf proceeds from her simple subject to develop a story with social and moral complications. The descendants

104

of the dead general, members of the Löwensköld family of Hedeby
manor, do not shy from any measures necessary to avenge the crime
against the general. They are responsible for the execution of three
peasants who are suspected of having the ring, but who are clearly
innocent. The ring is not recovered, and the dead general, who can
find no peace in his desecrated grave, continues to haunt Hedeby.
At the same time, a curse hangs heavy over the Löwensköld family
for having brought about an appalling miscarriage of justice.

This curse is brought down by the one person who remains to
look after the interests of the executed peasants, a woman named
Marit Eriksdotter, who because of the harsh judgment lost three
persons close to her, including her father and her fiancé. Marit, a
simple but clever woman, experienced in the art of healing, is
generally held in esteem by the people in the district. When she
learns one day, many years after the disappearance of the ring, that
the young son of Hedeby manor, Adrian Löwensköld, is near death
after a terrifying meeting with the ghost of the general, she rejoices
at the thought that the moment for revenge is at hand.

At this point, the typical Lagerlöf reversal takes place. Love enters
the picture, and the simple ghost story takes a new direction. The
Löwensköld housekeeper, a capable, efficient, and likable young girl
named Malvina Spaak, who has fallen in love with young Adrian,
goes of her own accord to Marit and begs her to save him. At first
the old woman refuses, but when she realizes the depth of the girl's
inconsolable sorrow, the memory of the love she once felt for her
fiancé is rekindled—a love cut short by death. For the sake of that
memory, Marit gives up thoughts of revenge and decides to help
the young people. It is within her power to bring peace to the ghost.
Years ago, she found the general's ring by chance, and now she sees
to it that it is returned to him. The gruesome task of returning the
ring to the general's grave she leaves to Malvina Spaak, who shudders
as the dead general snatches his prized possession from her when
she pushes it through a hole into the grave. At that very moment,
Adrian recovers.

There is, however, no happy ending to this story, which, in line
with the bitter view of life characteristic of the folktale, takes an
ironic turn. Just after Malvina happily witnesses Adrian's recovery,
she is quickly given to know that he is engaged to another, who,
as the story indicates, is of the same social class as he.

The gap between social classes that creates the bitter duality in
The General's Ring also determines the final resolution of the novel.
Not only has the lower class been treated unjustly, but now the
split between the Löwenskölds and the grievously wronged peasant
family of Marit becomes irreconcilable. The theme of sin unatoned
binds *The General's Ring* with the two other parts of the novel.

Family Guilt

Sin, punishment, revenge, and penance are themes that run
throughout Lagerlöf's entire literary production. They are connected
with her strong feeling for the unity of life; out of an awareness of
the kinship of all creatures, Lagerlöf developed an understanding
for the significance of each individual action. An outgrowth of this
sense of unity is the notion of family guilt. In *Jerusalem* and in *The
Outcast,* Lagerlöf treats this theme in an optimistic light. Individual
characters, by means of their good will, are able to overcome their
inheritance of evil.

In *The General's Ring,* on the other hand, the theme of the curse
is brought to a pessimistic conclusion. In *Anna Svärd,* the reader
learns that Marit, when she finds out that the Löwenskölds have
not fulfilled her wish to help Malvina Spaak find happiness in her
love for Adrian, places a curse on the aristocratic family: three
members of the family are doomed to a sudden and cruel end. An
eye for an eye and a tooth for a tooth. The instrument for revenge
is a false and intriguing woman named Thea Sundler, the daughter
of the Malvina Spaak who was so lamentably rejected by the fine
Löwensköld family. In one of the discarded manuscripts of the
trilogy, it is even explained that Thea is a reincarnated Marit—the
same woman who placed the curse on the family.[2] At the end of
Anna Svärd, Marit's prophecy is fulfilled, when the story returns to
Hedeby and Adrian Löwensköld, now a gloomy paterfamilias. He
and two other members of the family do indeed come to sudden
and cruel deaths. Marit's curse is carried out to the letter. But by
this time, the nemesis idea has become more of a mechanical device
for solving a complicated intrigue.

Charlotte Löwensköld

With the exception of their shared theme of family guilt, the
similarities between *The General's Ring* and the next volume of the
trilogy, *Charlotte Löwensköld* (1925), are few. These books clearly

bespeak Lagerlöf's versatility. She bases her first story on simple folktales of supernatural powers, using, appropriately, the speech of the common people to enliven her narrative, which is filled with examples of older folk superstitions. The language of *Charlotte Löwensköld,* on the other hand, is witty and at times sarcastic, a language that has the touch of a higher social class of the eighteenth century. While *The General's Ring* bears the heavy style of the folktale, *Charlotte Löwensköld* more closely follows the pattern of the fairy tale. But *Charlotte Löwensköld* is primarily a novel of intrigue in the true sense of the word—one with both comic and tragic elements, in which the interplay between the characters forms the core of the work; indeed, this interplay can even be seen as an end in itself.

There is, however, an ideological connection between the three parts of the trilogy, all of which treat the painful loss of happiness. *Charlotte Löwensköld* and *Anna Svärd* are Lagerlöf's most clearly defined love stories, in which the author has given free rein to her humoristic narrative style and her sharp satire—more so than with any of her works since *Gösta Berling's Saga.* Yet the situation in these novels is a tragic one, carried to its inevitable conclusion; these are stories of how hopes are frustrated by the success of evil, destructive plans and the failure of good intentions. There is a new fury in Lagerlöf's depiction of wickedness and evil; for example, the images she uses to describe the evil genius of these novels, the snakelike Thea Sundler, are filled with intense hatred. In some parts, fawning gossips and mendacity are treated with a ruthlessness scarcely observed before in her work.

The action of *Charlotte Löwensköld* takes place in Värmland around the 1830s. The setting no longer has the dimensions of *Gösta Berling's Saga,* however, but has been condensed to an idyllic rectory, the home of a happy old rector and his wife. In contrast to the younger characters in the novel, who are occupied with serious passions, they represent the humor and sound reasoning of comedy. Their foster daughter Charlotte is Lagerlöf's most charming female character. Unlike the ethereal young girls of the earlier works, she is witty and full of humor and vitality, as well as being sensitive and virtuous. As Elin Wägner put it, she is Lagerlöf as she herself wanted to be.[3] At the beginning of the novel, Charlotte is engaged to Karl Arthur Ekenstedt, the young and handsome, but poor, curate of the village, who is also a member of the Löwensköld family. The story concludes with the wedding of Charlotte and the rich foundry

owner Schagerström. Earlier, in the short story "Downie," Lagerlöf
depicted a similar abrupt change of partners. As in "Downie," the
fairy tale of Cinderella provides the basic theme—a poor girl attains
fame and fortune by becoming the mistress of a great manor. The
difference is that in "Downie" the girl also gets the man she loves;
in Charlotte Löwensköld, the girl loses her prince when she wins
wealth and honor. The different treatment of the theme is a clear
indication that Lagerlöf is moving away from her world of illusions.

Although *Charlotte Löwensköld* has an underlying fairy tale structure, it is essentially a novel in which the characters appear somewhat
like pieces in a game of chess. The narrative technique resembles
Jane Austen's manner of working within a strictly limited setting,
tracing step by step the various developments in a love story as if
they were moves on a chess board. Each new move made by one of
the characters is decisive for the game as a whole. Some of the moves
have momentous consequences.

Gradually, Charlotte is forced to retreat from her place at Karl
Arthur's side. Everything she does to regain the love of her fiancé
fails. Even her staunchest supporter, Karl Arthur's mother—Baroness Ekenstedt, a born Löwensköld and wife of Colonel Ekenstedt—
in whom she puts her trust, cannot help her. Actually, the mother's
relationship with her son is at the root of everything that happens.
Both *Charlotte Löwensköld* and *Anna Svärd* are novels that deal with
an overly strong mother dependency.

The baroness is described as an elegant woman of the world who
captivates everyone with her manner, charm, and tact. She is presented in such a strongly positive light that one scarcely notices the
criticism that Lagerlöf levels at her. The mother's exaggerated ideas
of her son's talents lay the groundwork for his later misfortune. She
wants to lead him to glittering heights that he is incapable of
reaching. But while the sins of the mother are merely indicated in
the text as underlying intentions, the resistance of the son, when
he attempts to free himself from her domination, is revealed in clear,
concrete situations. His first rebellion occurs when he chooses not
only to study theology but to embrace a world-denying pietism that
contrasts sharply with the views and the life of his mother, a woman
reared in the more light-hearted spirit of the worldly philosophy of
the Enlightenment. The son breaks mercilessly with the affluent,
happy, and culturally refined milieu of his childhood, represented

by his family home, and decides to lead an impoverished existence in the service of Jesus.

It has been emphasized previously that in the works of Lagerlöf, the fourth commandment is an especially important one. In the Löwensköld trilogy, the relationship of mother and son creates a dramatic register of emotions. The generation conflict is not solved by reconciliation, as it is in earlier works, but leads instead to destructiveness and dissolution. The mother falls ill and becomes an invalid when her son fails her. The son, in turn, becomes psychologically maimed; the repressed guilt he feels over the break with his mother renders him incapable of preaching. Lagerlöf's depiction of guilt undermining one's whole personality reveals her deep psychological insight.

Charlotte is Karl Arthur's good genius, the joy of his life, but she is essentially on his mother's side. She is, in a sense, a younger version of the charming Baroness Ekenstedt, with the significant difference that she is neither rich nor spoiled. Nor is she afraid of sharing the curate's dream of an unpretentious life. Yet her strong devotion to Karl Arthur's mother influences her, causing her to steer him in the direction his mother wants him to take. The relationship between Charlotte and the older woman is tender and trusting, marked by worshipful admiration on the part of the younger woman. Is it perhaps her future mother-in-law that Charlotte really loves?

Since the text gives only a hint that Charlotte, like the baroness, exerts pressure on Karl Arthur and assumes a guardianship over him of the kind he wants to free himself of, the reader is made all the more aware of Karl Arthur's stupidity and lack of reason when he regards Charlotte as an instrument of temptation, determined to lead him to damnation. His sudden decision to break with her and go out on the highway to let "God choose" his future bride—he intends to marry the first girl who crosses his path—is proof of his lack of reason. Yet the text also allows the interpretation that he has a legitimate and desperate need to escape from the all-too-domineering women who have been directing his life. While Karl Arthur's behavior may be rash—and basically cynical—it certainly should not be construed as entirely negative, not if one understands Lagerlöf's views regarding the importance of external forces in determining people's lives. The young curate opposes all other schemes and all social pressures with his plan to be guided by superhuman powers.

To a certain extent, Karl Arthur's idea of having God choose a wife for him turns out well. The girl he meets on the road is Anna Svärd, a young, beautiful peasant girl from Dalecarlia, who wears the colorful costume of her home parish. Anna earns her living as an itinerant peddler. With her, Karl Arthur plans to begin a new life in the service of Christ; he dreams that he will find paradise by leading a simple, unpretentious existence in a little gray cottage.

But the snake in the paradise, Thea Sundler, makes sure that his dream does not come true. Karl Arthur believes that he is following the will of God, but he is instead fulfilling the most ardent wishes of Thea Sundler. She binds the young, handsome curate to her and sees to it that he breaks with those who have his best interests at heart. Her evil designs prevent the reconciliation with Karl Arthur that Charlotte so desperately yearns for and tries to bring about.

Charlotte Löwensköld deals not only with the fateful consequences of human acts and feelings, but also with the inability of human beings to see themselves and others as they really are. In line with the formula of the fairy tale, their lives are determined by powers over which they have no control. Also, as in the fairy tale, good and evil are sharply polarized. Against Charlotte, the good angel, stands Thea, described with merciless irony, who represents in pure form the romantic and unrealistic character traits that make Karl Arthur somewhat attractive. In the case of Thea, these qualities reflect only a falseness. She is characterized in metaphorical language, in which the words *snake* and *toad* are prominent. Her own speech is strikingly reminiscent of romantic poetry. Lagerlöf cruelly parodies her emotional drivel, which the more rational inhabitants of the rectory joke about, but which is completely in accord with Karl Arthur's otherworldliness. Thea "was a romantic from the top of her head to the balls of her feet."

Thea gradually separates Charlotte and Karl Arthur, snaring him in her trap. As the one relationship deteriorates, however, another begins to develop; Charlotte, the poor girl of the rectory, soon becomes permanently linked with the richest and most powerful man in the district, the foundry owner Schagerström, whose life story, which contrasts sharply with that of Karl Arthur, is summarized in a few retrospective chapters. As a child he was picked on because he was so ugly; even his mother rejected him. While

Karl Arthur is raised as a prince in a fairy tale, Schagerström is the tale's changeling, who in the end is, nevertheless, rescued by a princess. In other words, he marries a rich and charming heiress and becomes master of her empire of iron foundries. When she dies, he decides, in his despair, to abandon his responsibilities, but before long his sense of duty returns, and he resumes his role as manager of the foundries.

Schagerström represents practical life. He has arrived at his position, not only through marriage, but also through realism and hard work. Yet he lives in a stately, romantic manor. One day his circumstances prompt him to gaze upon the poor but enchanting Charlotte, and before long he travels to the rectory to seek her hand in marriage. At first he meets with a contemptuous refusal; he should have known that she was engaged to another. But by means of a series of meetings and misunderstandings, the action moves in a direction that none of those involved could have imagined. Schagerström's second proposal receives an affirmative answer.

The plot of *Charlotte Löwensköld* is sometimes excessively contrived. On the surface, the story appears to be a light comedy. The novel, with its many humorous and satirical scenes, is wittier and more comical than any of Lagerlöf's other works. But below the surface lies a story of failed hopes, wasted dreams, and trust that comes to nought.

Even if the plot is occasionally far-fetched, the novel has a vitality that arises from its portrayal of the emotional ups and downs of its main character. Charlotte's love and sorrow give the story its inner tension. She seeks for signs that will indicate the direction her life should take—a life in which she feels like "a captive prisoner," like one dominated by "witchcraft." Finally, she convinces herself that she must sacrifice her own personal happiness in order that the young curate will be able to play the role of spiritual hero he dreams of. The immediate consequences of her sacrifice prove to her that she was right, for Karl Arthur suddenly achieves success in the village. Through his sermons, he becomes a real leader of the people and instigates a religious revival. He also impresses the entire community by performing a grand humanitarian act. In a magnanimous gesture, he takes in a group of orphans about to be auctioned off as servants to people in the village, promising to take care of them himself.

While Karl Arthur's path appears to be on the way to its zenith, Charlotte's star is descending. Once again, in connection with Charlotte, Lagerlöf takes up the theme of being ostracized. In the small community where the young girl from the rectory lives, gossip flourishes and creeps about like a slimy snake. When the rumor originates that she has rejected the curate in order to catch a rich man, Charlotte is subjected to open scorn. Yet to prevent any suspicion from falling upon the man she loves, she does nothing to justify herself. Like many of her sisters in other Lagerlöf stories, she becomes a saint and martyr. On one occasion, even the image of Christ crucified is related to her character. Here, as in many other instances, Lagerlöf employs a Biblical allusion to accentuate the psychological situation.

Charlotte's sacrifice is perhaps greater than those made by her counterparts in other works. She renounces love and happiness in order to help the man she loves and his mother. Underlying this sacrifice is a bargain, a conspiracy customarily found in older novels of intrigue. Charlotte persuades Thea Sundler to go along with a plan to reconcile Karl Arthur with his mother. In return, Charlotte promises to marry Schagerström as soon as possible; this reassures Thea that, in the future, Charlotte will have no more influence on Karl Arthur.

Everything seems to go according to plan. Charlotte marries the rich foundry owner, and Karl Arthur goes home to re-establish his relationship with his mother. But his trip is disastrous. Under the influence of Thea, Karl Arthur demands an apology from his mother. In her overwhelming anger and disappointment, she suffers a stroke, and he is cast out of his family home forever. When Charlotte tearfully reflects on this unfortunate situation, she blames herself for not understanding that Karl Arthur still bore resentment toward his mother and that, consequently, a reconciliation was impossible.

As the intrigue continues to develop, determined mainly by Thea's evil intentions, one detects the psychological dynamics that underlie all these disastrous events. Karl Arthur's main problem is his dependence on his mother (and on Charlotte), which undercuts his ability to find his own identity. The love and the authority of these two women make demands upon him that he, weak and limited as he is, cannot fulfill. The women, in turn, are unable to understand his real character; their overestimation of his abilities cause him great distress. (The more realistic view of Karl Arthur is represented by the old rector and his wife.) In the midst of the strongly negative and critical depiction of the young curate, the story offers an explanation for his flight into romantic ecstasies and dreams of freedom. Lagerlöf tells of the flight from reality in an earlier story, *The Emperor of Portugallia,* in which she shows considerably more sympathy for the protagonist. Karl Arthur does not actually become mentally ill, as does the main character in the earlier work, but only rarely is he capable of taking an objective look at his own existence and understanding the forces that determine it.

All things considered, *Charlotte Löwensköld* ends on an optimistic and harmonious note—at least with regard to Charlotte herself. Her wedding with Schagerström is described as a jovial party, and the bride enters her new role with happiness and ambition. Although her marriage is not based on romantic love, Charlotte nevertheless becomes, in a sense, a princess. On one level, then, the Cinderella theme is brought to its proper conclusion. At the same time, however, Charlotte—to a much greater degree than Lagerlöf's other young female protagonists—is bold and enterprising; moreover, she has certain characteristics in common with the tomboys in girls' stories. In contrast to these heroines, however, Charlotte takes the initiative in her sexual relationship with her husband. In his deep consideration for his bride, who he knows does not love him, Schagerström is prepared to release her from her marital obligations. In the Löwensköld cycle, Lagerlöf has become so modern that she refers to sexual relations in the case of Charlotte and Schagerström, as well as in the case of Karl Arthur and Anna Svärd.

The final solution in *Charlotte Löwensköld,* which concentrates on the practical aspects of life, may point to the fact that Lagerlöf has now come to terms with the life of dreams and fantasy that she had been examining critically ever since *Gösta Berling's Saga.* The world of illusions and beautiful phrases receives a hard blow when it is parodied in Thea Sundler's emotionality and Karl Arthur's romantic rejection of worldly things. Yet in Lagerlöf, romanticism is never placed one-sidedly in contrast to realism; for example, while Charlotte certainly stands with both feet on the ground—indeed, compared with Thea she appears almost ruthlessly level-headed—she still has her shares of idealism and imagination. Nor is Charlotte's love dead; in fact, one can find in *Anna Svärd* one of the most beautiful hymns to love ever written by Lagerlöf in a passage in which Charlotte, reminiscing on the days when she was in love with Karl Arthur, recalls how she once danced for sheer joy like a fairy on a summer night.

In *Charlotte Löwensköld* and *Anna Svärd*, more clearly than in any of her works, Lagerlöf has given expression to her never fulfilled dream of love, that which originated in the imagination of a teenager. With Charlotte's idealism, born out of love, she richly illustrates the readiness to sacrifice everything for a loved one that she was to write about some years later in *The Diary of Selma Lagerlöf*. Perhaps, too, she is expressing her own disappointment over thwarted hopes in her tale of the life of the girl from the rectory. But Lagerlöf apparently had other dreams, one of which surely was the romantic idea to live with one she loved in a little gray cottage—in any case, the cottage appears in various places throughout her literary works. Another dream was to be mistress over a great estate, a role which, in part, she was able to play, and which she gives to Charlotte Löwensköld, the most charming of all her female protagonists.

Anna Svärd

Anna Svärd, which continues immediately where *Charlotte Löwensköld* leaves off, deals primarily with the wedding and the marriage of Karl Arthur and his beautiful peasant girl from Dalecarlia. The gap between the ill-matched pair has both its comic and its tragic aspects. The Dalecarlian girl dreams of carefree days at a rich rectory; the young curate, essentially the spoiled son of rich parents, yearns for poverty and simplicity. While Anna, who loves her husband, makes the best of her life in the little gray cottage that he has chosen for their home, her husband gets the worst of it.

Anna Svärd traces Karl Arthur's path to destruction and collapse. His story is based on actual documented material, correspondence from the beginning of the nineteenth century, which Lagerlöf had access to, that tells the story of a student named Estenberg. He began his studies with high hopes, but his life ended in failure and despair. Lagerlöf became absorbed in the psychological puzzle of his story. In a letter she describes the actual background of Karl Arthur in the following manner:

There was once a young clergyman who quarreled with his fiancée and then went out and proposed to a Dalecarlian girl, the first woman he met, and married her. This caused a quarrel with his parents, and he was disinherited. Little by little, he went downhill, fell into the hands of an ingratiating, flattering woman, and at the end died a pauper at the home of his Dalecarlian wife, who had returned to her home village and, with vigor and efficiency, managed to secure for herself a good economic position.[4]

The letter provided the outline for the story of Karl Arthur and Anna Svärd. The heroine develops into a vital and complex figure, a new type of woman in Lagerlöf's oeuvre, the only one who is independent. She earns her own living and has complete confidence in her own authority. She takes upon herself all the practical activities that belong to the simple life. The reader's sympathies are drawn to Anna, even though one perceives the author's sympathy for the young curate when his elevated thoughts are disturbed by the constant thumping of his wife's weaving loom.

As a representative for feminism, Anna Svärd is so modern that she renders her husband superfluous. He is described as a troublesome person in the cottage where his wife and the ten children he took home from the auction lead a strenuous but happy existence. Their life is depicted in a long chapter bearing the ironic title "Paradise." The next chapter is called "The Fall." Thus the stages of the marriage follow the paradise myth. The snake, in the form of Thea, tempts Karl Arthur to treat Anna shamefully, crushing all her hopes. Just as he repudiated his mother and Charlotte, he now rejects Anna, who not only loves him, but also possesses the necessary qualities that allow them and their adopted children to survive in their impoverished circumstances. With a strong ironic tone, Lagerlöf tells how Karl Arthur, the young curate who had yearned to live among the common people, essentially disdains his wife and her household activities. The final expulsion from paradise takes place when the husband sends the children away. This deed, of course, is also one planned by Thea Sundler. When Anna, now expecting a child of her own, is deprived of her other responsibilities and the happiness the children bring her, she leaves the cottage and Karl Arthur. Thea is triumphant. Finally, Karl Arthur belongs completely to her!

When the curate collects himself after the shock of Anna's disappearance, he experiences a wonderful feeling of freedom. Now he can finally realize his dream to become a poor man of God, connected to no church; he wants to become an itinerant preacher, a preacher of the marketplace who will seek his congregation at fairs and other places where people gather. What he longs for is a life without any ties. "Wife, home, the respect of the community—all these meant nothing to him on the path he had chosen to tread."

Karl Arthur's goal appears as an antithesis to the ideal that Lagerlöf once depicted in the agrarian values of Ingmar Ingmarsson, with his strong sense of responsibility for keeping up the family home, traditions, and respectability. Karl Arthur's joy over his newly gained freedom appears almost as a caricature of the idea, held by the sons of Ingmar, that they walk in the ways of God. Karl Arthur and Thea appear all the more grotesque, as they travel forth with their wagon to save people. They appear, with their songs and sermons, in the midst of the noisy festivities of country fairs. Soon, however, their relationship begins to sour, when they direct their inner aggression toward each other.

Lagerlöf's interest in destructive personalities can be traced back to *Gösta Berling's Saga*. But never before has she described human degradation with a naturalism so free of illusions as she does in *Anna Svärd*, in which she depicts both the inner and outer decline of Karl Arthur and Thea.

When it comes to unmasking demons and angels, *Anna Svärd* contains scenes that belong to the best in all of Lagerlöf's literary works. While the tone of the novel is considerably gloomier than that of *Charlotte Löwensköld*, there are also humorous and satirical elements present; some of the episodes have a stinging quality never seen before in Lagerlöf's works. Manifestations of love are described in a variety of ways, most grippingly in the story of Karl Arthur's mother, the baroness, who partially loses her memory after her stroke, forgetting her rift with her son and sinking completely into thoughts of the old, loving relationship she once enjoyed with him. With tender irony, Lagerlöf describes how her daughter—whom the mother never cared much about—must dutifully read aloud to her over and over the letters Karl Arthur wrote home when he was a student.

Because the paths of Anna Svärd and Karl Arthur part, the novel, too, gradually becomes divided into the separate stories of their lives—to such an extent that it appears impossible for the threads of action to be brought together again and the story wound up. The conclusion is indeed weak and melodramatic, contrived so that the curse that hangs over the Löwensköld family is finally fulfilled. Three members of the family lose their lives in fatal accidents—one freezes to death after his sledge turns over on him, and two fall through a hole in the ice and drown. Karl Arthur, however, also related to the Löwenskölds, manages to escape with his life, even though he too is out on the ice at the time of the fateful drowning. Originally, Lagerlöf had planned to have him die too, and that perhaps would have been best. Instead, however, she sends him as a missionary to Africa, where he receives his baptism of fire in a land of genuine poverty and privation. At the end of the novel, Karl Arthur returns home after eight years as a missionary. He enters Anna Svärd's cottage, where she has managed very well for herself since his disappearance. The book ends with a question: How will she receive him?

The reader never finds out. During the 1930s, Lagerlöf attempted to complete the story of her hero in a fourth part, which she entitled *Karl-Artur Ekenstedt (Karl Arthur Ekenstedt)*.[5] Judging from the manuscript, the book was to be about his penance and reconciliation. But the work did not progress, perhaps because the author's opinion of her protagonist had sunk too low. There is nothing in the negatively drawn character on which a credible positive development can be based.

Around Christmas of 1930, *The General's Ring, Charlotte Löwensköld,* and *Anna Svärd* were published in America in one volume entitled *The Ring of the Löwenskölds,* which enjoyed an extraordinary reception. "Every day I receive requests for autographs, portraits, etc.," Lagerlöf was pleased to write her friend Henriette Coyet (letter of 17 February 1931). She points out too that "it has been terribly difficult" for her books "to gain acceptance in the Anglo-Saxon world," although they were somewhat more successful in the United States than in England. Lagerlöf certainly had received good reviews earlier, for example, for *Mårbacka,* which appeared in the United States in 1924,[6] but it was clearly the Löwensköld trilogy that assured her fame in America.

Chapter Eight

Selma Lagerlöf and the Role of Writer

Lagerlöf's Literary Program

Lagerlöf was, in the true sense of the word, a storyteller and a creator of living characters. In letters and interviews, she often stressed that she was a listener and observer, but "not one of those who themselves play a significant role on life's stage."[1] According to Lagerlöf, she was happy to remain on the "spectator's bench and then later tell about what others were good enough to experience," but she herself did not play a particularly interesting role in life.[2]

Elin Wägner objects to this self-description by suggesting that Lagerlöf was, without a doubt, much more "knowledgeable about the turbulent game of life than a mere spectator watching from the grandstand could possibly be."[3] While this is true, it is nevertheless interesting that Lagerlöf uses the traditional metaphor of life as a stage upon which all carry out their roles. It has been pointed out in the previous chapters that this role playing is an underlying idea in her work. She depicts people in an ever-shifting interplay of roles and relationships, with an understanding of the many possibilities for self-realization that life offers.

The most fruitful sources of information about Lagerlöf's thoughts on various questions are her interviews and letters. This also holds true in the question of how she regards her role and her task as a writer. Letters from the Gösta Berling years, primarily the correspondence with Sophie Adlersparre, are of special interest. What is striking in these letters is Lagerlöf's basic aesthetic view, which she was to hold for the rest of her life. In her literary work, she seeks beauty above all. The idea of the poetic and of poeticizing is characteristic of her purpose as an author. "My task is to bring out the poetically beautiful from even the most shabby situation," she explained to Sophie Adlersparre (21 February 1891). The hero of her first novel is called "Gösta Berling, poet," because his task is to sow "gold dust over the gray fabric of life." On one occasion, he appeals directly to those around him, telling them that it is better to build castles in the air in one's imagination than to devote oneself to the architecture of reality:

> The pyramids weigh heavy upon the earth, the tower of Babel has pierced through the sky, the beautiful temples and the gray fortresses have risen out of the dust. But of all that human hands have built, is there anything that has not fallen or will not fall? O mankind, cast away your trowels and bricks! Spread the mason's apron over your heads and lay yourselves down to build the beautiful castle of dreams! What has the spirit to do with temples of stone and brick? Learn to build eternal castles of dreams and visions! (from the chapter "The Young Countess" in *Gösta Berling's Saga*)

These words, of course, should not be taken too seriously, for they are spoken by Gösta Berling, the genuine representative of joy and beauty. But this frivolous exhortation is perhaps in line with the propaganda against naturalism which began to appear at the end of the 1880s. In his manifesto "Renaissance" (1889), Verner von Heidenstam attacked with biting irony photographic realism, which he called "shoemaker realism," and pleaded for imagination and idealism under the motto: "Let us rush into literary adventure!" He also rejects everyday realism as a norm for poetry and fiction in "Pepitas bröllop" ("Pepita's Wedding"), a manifesto he and the critic Oscar Levertin published in 1890. Von Heidenstam and Levertin further call for a new perspective on reality that includes imagination, aesthetic sensitivity, and individualism, asking, "Are the fantasies of a writer not also a form of reality?" Gösta Berling's exhortation to build dream castles might have been taken from "Pepita's Wedding," for there, too, art is compared to a church, which ought to have room for "the sparkling mosaics created by a sense of beauty, based on gold and crowned with the imagination, airily rising to the heights."[4]

Oscar Levertin immediately saw in *Gösta Berling's Saga* an expression for the new aesthetics that he and Heidenstam were promoting. Surprised and impressed by the work, he characterized it as "the first work in accordance with the Heidenstam-Levertin aesthetics." This accord, however, he believed to be coincidental. The author of *Gösta Berling's Saga* was, for him, "a little school ma'am, a little one, who has never been outside the boundaries of Sweden, but who has lived alone and has a whole forgotten and concealed provincial mysticism inside her."[5] From the very beginning, Levertin regarded Lagerlöf as a naive writer—the word *little,* for example, appears twice in the quoted passage—and he does not even ask whether she might have been influenced by the contemporary literary debate.

Lagerlöf scholars have finally changed this picture created by Levertin of the author of *Gösta Berling's Saga.* It is true that Lagerlöf, unlike her male colleagues, had not yet made any journeys abroad. Nor had she taken part in drawing up a literary manifesto or been a member of a literary coterie. But she had completed her own important course of education, was very well read at an early age, and had developed her own independent aesthetic ideas. She was interested in the main writers and thinkers of her time, such as Strindberg, Darwin, Spencer, Ibsen, and Georg Brandes.[6] Since she always kept abreast of literary developments, one can assume with assurance that she was acquainted with the new impulses in literature around 1890, which presaged that naturalism—the naturalism that had to do with depiction of everyday life and photographic realism—was becoming increasingly less significant in its role as determiner of literary norms.

Throughout her life, Lagerlöf generally adhered to the literary practice that she had established during her work on *Gösta Berling's Saga.* There is much clear evidence of this; for example, in a letter of 1921, Lagerlöf, greatly irritated, complains about people who want her to take action in various situations:

I am not a person of action; I want to tell about the great achievements of others. I was created to see, to narrate, to meditate, and to change into poetry that which life offers. (letter to Kajsa Hansen, 13 August 1921)

The fact that Lagerlöf strives for an aesthetic ideal does not mean that she takes an exclusive stance distant from everyday life. On the contrary, she is more of a realist than many writers who are called realists. She had a distinct visual gift, had, as someone expressed it, a strong camera. "For her, imagination was, in a peculiar way, substantiated by the experience of reality," writes the Lagerlöf scholar Gunnar Ahlström, who adds, "Realism and truth were no abstract concepts for this imaginative artist, but the basic premises for her narrative art."[7]

As has been pointed out, Lagerlöf's stories rarely developed out of pure imagination; they had, rather, a clear basis in a story she read or heard, a newspaper article, or some other report. Almost everything she wrote can be traced to such a source, which her imagination helped her reshape. Imagination is also the means by which she interpreted existence. This she explained herself in the following clear and simple manner: "If I can grasp a little bit of reality and change it into poetry, I am satisfied."[8] In this case, poetry means fiction.

Lagerlöf's aesthetic program also included a social attitude and purpose that impart to it an almost didactic function: "I want to teach people the art of bringing a glimmer of beauty into the most simple life."[9] She explained that she wanted, with *Gösta Berling's Saga,* to do something for the tired and work-worn people in her home village. "I wanted the people up there to accept the book as my gift to them in return for the richness of expression and enjoyment that their memory has given me."[10] But it is clear that her aim went far beyond the desire to be a village writer. She wanted to make a contribution to the national literature of Sweden. In a confident moment, she declared that *Gösta Berling's Saga* was something that "the country and the people" needed.[11]

Lagerlöf as Popular Writer

Even when she was working on *Gösta Berling's Saga,* Lagerlöf expressed an ardent wish that she might become a writer for broad audiences. She hoped, she said, that the book would be a genuine *folkbok*—or work of popular literature—a notion that she later came to apply to several of her works. As she wrote to her friend in Landskrona, Elise Malmros, she wanted to approach "the large public, which does not judge, but seizes that which takes its fancy, no matter what the artistic value may be." She herself suggested that she was unusual in her strong interest in the reactions of ordinary people: "Have you ever before heard of a writer who places more value on the judgement of children and servants than on that of professional critics?" But, she confessed, "if I, with all my peculiarities, could be a writer of the people, I would be very glad—no, not glad, but most seriously happy" (letter of 22 February 1891). One should, however, take with a grain of salt the following outpourings: "I have always felt that it would be all right if the scholars and critics attacked me, as long as I had the people on my side. I want my public to consist of young people and country folk."[12]

Gradually, she did indeed achieve her purpose—her books became popular works. With *Jerusalem,* she received great acclaim from critics as well as from the general reading public. But when the reviews for the second part of the novel were less than enthusiastic, she pointed out with satisfaction on several occasions that she still enjoyed the favor of her readers.

The huge success of her books among the general public rested also on the fact that they came out in inexpensive editions soon after they were published; even the working class could afford to buy them. In addition, she reached a wide public because of her openness to new media. She sometimes spoke on the radio with a strikingly beautiful voice. In 1933, a year of international crisis, she addressed a radio speech to America, in which she appealed to "the great daughterland in the West" to dispel the oppressive darkness in the world.[13] She was also very much interested in the films that were being made of her books. Several of them are considered, even on an international scale, to be gems of the silent film; their popularity gained her scores of new readers. Now, in the 1980s, television producers are discovering that her literary works are a veritable gold mine for television drama.

There were, of course, other reasons—and deeper ones—for Lagerlöf's popularity than merely the extensive distribution of her works. Ultimately, it rested on her choice of subjects, themes, and styles. Her interest in original narratives, in myths, folktales, fairy tales, and legends led her to delve into the depths of the folk culture. Yet, even though anonymous folk literature was one of her main sources, she often received inspiration from contemporary materials. She was an avid newspaper reader, and the daily newspapers provided her with material for many a story. During her visit to Italy, for example, she absorbed more than the legends of the regions she visited; her reading of newspapers also left its traces in the short stories, as well as in the novel *The Miracles of Antichrist.* (It should perhaps be mentioned that she had a good reading knowledge of Italian.)

In her choice of subjects, Lagerlöf preferred to seek the unknown, that which disclosed a certain primordiality, something primitive or puzzling. As one Lagerlöf scholar expressed it, she had an "unusual

eye for unexploited and artistically fruitful themes."[14] She understood what possibilities a theme might offer, though it be concealed
in an anecdote, a ghost story, a letter, a newspaper, or a half-
forgotten old book. In this lies the basis for her development as a
popular writer.

The question whether her writing style marks her as a popular
writer is more complicated. From oral narrative, she doubtless learned
to treat a story in a way that maintained its interest. The tension
in her stories builds uninterruptedly to a climax, which often brings
about a reversal of the situation. The conclusion is always carefully
anticipated, but it nevertheless appears unexpected. An important
aspect of her narrative technique is that she conceived her stories as
being read aloud.

Fairy tales and folktales helped her develop her naive narrative
stance—the simple, direct manner of presentation that makes her
literary works accessible to all. The chapter on her short stories
points out how she employed both of these basic models—the optimistic fairy tale, in which the hero is victorious over the dragons
of existence, and the pessimistic folktale, in which man succumbs
to the powers. Also, with regard to composition, language, and
style, folk literature was a source of inspiration for her writing.
Personification and animism are prominent characteristics in her
world of narrative, as they are in a fairy tale. Moreover, everything
is living and animated.

The Bible, which constituted a common frame of reference for
people of Lagerlöf's day, was also an important source of inspiration
for her. Its influence can be seen in connection with myths, special
motifs and symbols, and, to the greatest degree, in the language.
Lagerlöf's general view of existence as a journey in an atmosphere of suffering, and often penitence, has its primary source in
the images and ideas of the New Testament. The importance of the
Christ figure for her writing has often been pointed out, perhaps
even exaggerated, for Lagerlöf's own view was not essentially
Christocentric.[15]

Contrasting with Biblical elements, the influence of old Icelandic
literature, another important model for her creative work, occasionally breaks through in a most effective manner. The strict fa-
talism of old Norse literature—found also, incidentally, in folk
literature—is confronted with New Testament ideas of mercy and
reconciliation, the notions of human good will and the capacity for

love—powers that can alter an evil, destructive situation. Lagerlöf's stories are, on the whole, based on the strong contrasting forces of opposing values—for example, revenge and love or sin and justice. *The Treasure* is a typical example of a story charged by all these conflicting elements. At the same time, the Icelandic saga also contributes structurally to the linearity and clarity, not only of that story, but of several others as well—*Jerusalem*, for example.

The Highly Conscious Artist

Lagerlöf, however, is not a popular writer in the sense that she adapts her fiction to the needs and desires of the masses. Current research has emphasized more and more that although her stories are rooted in folk tradition, her narrative technique demonstrates clearly that she is by no means a simple and primitive writer, but a highly conscious artist. This can be seen especially in the composition of her individual novels, in which the structural design— the arrangement of individual chapters, each complete in itself, into a richly diversified causal relationship—demands a high degree of control over the material and ability to structure a narrative. In *Gösta Berling's Saga,* Lagerlöf does not quite achieve complete structural unity, but *Jerusalem* offers an example of a novelistic structure in which each individual episode is a complete story in itself and at the same time an integral part of an ingenious collective plan.

The role of the narrator and the narrative perspective varies in Lagerlöf's works. In some, the narrator plays a major role, introducing and commenting on the story. The first-person narrator in *Gösta Berling's Saga,* for example, creates a special mood, with his passionate outcries and lyrically accented commentary. In other works, the narrator tells the story in a more intimate style, playing the role of cultural intermediary, as, for example, in The *Ring of the Löwenskölds.* Occasionally, there is no explicit narrator. Certain stories are told simply and directly; others are based primarily on insight into the thoughts of the characters.

Lagerlöf's stories often involve a sophisticated alternation between the narrated moment and the depiction of the scenic background. On the whole, the dramatic element in her fiction is very clear. Her inclusion of tragic irony and extreme reversals in the lives of her characters is more reminiscent of the drama of classical antiquity and the Ibsenesque drama than of the folktale. Still, Lagerlöf was no dramatist; the many attempts made, by herself and others, to adapt her novels for the stage were seldom successful.

In certain stories, Lagerlöf adds an observer, a sort of *raisonneur,* who comments on the action. Torarin, the fishmonger in *The Treasure,* is such a figure, as is Lilljänta in *Liliecrona's Home,* the little girl who tries to interpret the tragic events at Lövdala. These characters play a similar role to that of the reader, but since their interpretation of what happens is naive and incomplete, the reader himself is also challenged to work intensively with problems in the text. Although the role of the reader in Lagerlöf's fiction is definitely very important, no attention has, as yet, been paid to it.

Characteristic of Lagerlöf's narrative method is her manner of allowing for various perspectives and ways of interpreting a story and then leaving it up to her readers to take a position regarding the questions presented. Her characters represent not only different standpoints. Frequently they also come from different social classes and speak different kinds of language. In *The Emperor of Portugallia,* for example, the tenant farmers speak a language colored by dialect, and the people of the manor speak cultivated Swedish. One scholar, Erland Lagerroth, has described Lagerlöf's books as dialogue-novels. [16] He also applies the term *polyphonic novel* to some of her works. Lagerlöf's is the voice that "gives voice to the voices." [17] The polyphonic elements may be the basis for all narrative literature, especially in its original Homeric meaning of creating an objective picture of reality.

Another feature of Lagerlöf's art that is beginning to attract attention is the often strong discrepancy between what is on the surface and what lies beneath it in her works. On the surface, the stories can appear artless and simple, but upon closer scrutiny they reveal a complicated structure. The question is whether the similarities with the popular narrative extend deeper than the superficial level of the action. The correspondence between the qualities of popular naive literature and the literature of high culture gives Lagerlöf's work its distinctive stamp. Her method is to turn a simple folk motif into a narrative with many different psychological dimensions. One can also assert, however, that psychological developments are shaped into concrete stories patterned after the dramatic structure of folk literature. [18]

To the complex and artistic qualities of Lagerlöf's works belongs also her symbolic language. In an allegorical way, she uses nature myths and other popular tales as images of the powers of existence. As it has been pointed out, in *Gösta Berling's Saga* there is a wealth of personification of various feelings and attitudes, from "the spirit with the icy eyes" to the Dovre witch. The symbolic figure who etches herself most strongly in the reader's memory is, however, Lady Sorrow in *The Tale of a Manor,* the woman with wings made of leather patches, a dream figure, created in a moment of strong inspiration. [19]

On the whole, the ability to mythify existence pervades Lagerlöf's narrative practice. While her characters have distinct social roots, they are, nevertheless, ultimately representatives of various attitudes toward life. Since people have, as a rule, applied the demands of naturalism to Lagerlöf's art, they often have been blind to her method of using a complex interplay of roles, related to each other, to cultivate and analyze humanity in all its forms—from the most wild and uncivilized to the ethereally pure and saintlike. Perhaps the secret of her distinction as a popular writer lies in this exploration of "the soul, that vast country" to which we all belong. [20] As Elin Wägner expresses it, she possessed the ability to "touch with her words something common to human beings all over the world." [21]

The Writer and the Message

Even if Lagerlöf gave expression to many voices on life's stage, she often stressed the important role of the writer's own personality, for it is that which determines the ability of a work of fiction to affect others. While working on *Gösta Berling's Saga,* she became aware of how ruthlessly she could indulge in self-exploitation in moments of inspiration, an act she described as writing "as I am in the very depths of my soul." Eventually, she became Sweden's most imitated writer. This irritated her and she even wrote to a writer who imitated her style that it was not the stories in themselves that readers were interested in, but the writer's ego that presided over the work and the personality reflected in that work. [22]

At the same time, however, she rejected the role of writer *engagé,* stressing that she wanted to avoid sermonizing. She was careful to point out her independence, especially in connection with religious matters. She was disposed toward skepticism and doubt. Statements found in two letters written at different times illustrate her attempts to defend herself against those who wanted her to choose sides:

I have had periods when I have been a strong materialist and a woman of reason, but my temperament as an author, wanting to move in the field of mysticism, always forces me back into the ranks of believers. So you find widely differing opinions in my works. . . . I am afraid you will soon find that my mind is a room where all instruments play, but the basic melody is missing. (letter to Valfrid Vasenius, 4 April 1909)

and

I belong to those silly hens that go around picking grains in all fields until they don't know where they belong. If I ever had a deep religious experience, I should probably know where I belong. (letter to Stella Rydholm, 17 September 1923)

In 1932, a study of Lagerlöf appeared which places great stress on the ideological and social tendentiousness in her work. The book, by Stellan Arvidson, occasioned a correspondence between the author, Arvidson, and Lagerlöf, in which Lagerlöf makes several interesting statements about her method and her intentions as a writer. On the whole, she reacted favorably to the book. Arvidson makes the important observation that ever since her first novel, her works have been stamped by a social commitment and supported by ideas reflected in the issues of the times. Still, Lagerlöf had certain objections to his argument, pointing out that he believed too much in the writer's preliminary design for her work:

It has always been the case, for me at least, that a novel has grown from a tiny seed, and then the stem, branches, and leaves developed gradually, until the tree was finished, but there was never any design, such as one draws up for a building. I think that the whole work becomes more credible when it grows in this manner and is not built up, more like nature's own work. (4 April 1932)

In another letter, she explains in the same spirit that she allowed the subject she chose to grow "and develop the greatest possible clarity and beauty, without thinking so much about rules and aesthetics" (5 December 1933).

Lagerlöf as Feminist Author

In his study of Lagerlöf's ideas, Stellan Arvidson also takes up her relationship to feminism, stressing that she "above all depicted the lives of women and showed woman's role in the home and in society"—an assertion that in itself invites objection.[23]

When Lagerlöf made her debut as a novelist, the novel had already been established as a genre for women writers; readers, too, may have been predominantly women. The nineteenth century was a golden age for female prose writers. One need only think of the many brilliant English women writers—the Brontës, Jane Austen, and George Eliot, for example. In Sweden, Fredrika Bremer had gained considerable fame. By the 1880s, when Lagerlöf was becoming seriously interested in women's questions, Sweden claimed a large circle of women writers, all realists.

What importance did Lagerlöf's being a woman have for her role as an author? It is significant that she began her literary career just when the feminist movement started to gain real momentum in Sweden. From the beginning, she was supported by women interested in her work, who helped her both with money and encouragement. As has been mentioned, it was a feminist, Eva Fryxell, who convinced her to leave her parental home and get an education. She also had a devoted helper in Sophie Adlersparre, the strong-willed founder of the Fredrika Bremer Society, who with great enthusiasm—occasionally, perhaps, with too much authority—followed the genesis of *Gösta Berling's Saga*. Lagerlöf published her first literary works, both lyric poetry and prose, in *Dagny*, the journal of the Fredrika Bremer Society, and when it came to writing *Gösta Berling's Saga* and then introducing the novel to the public, she received special support from the feminist movement in both Denmark and Sweden.

Did Lagerlöf, in turn, come to be important for feminism? It is clear that she never played as active a role in the feminist debate as did Fredrika Bremer or her well-known contemporary, Ellen Key. She also explained explicitly that she primarily wanted to serve feminism "indirectly," in the same manner that she brought out her other ideological messages.[24] There was one question, however, in which Lagerlöf did become so involved that she stepped forth publicly as an agitator—the question of women's suffrage, a reform not carried out in Sweden until 1919. By that time, the women's suffrage movement, which Lagerlöf engaged in, had been active for a few decades. In 1911, the World Congress for Women's Suffrage was organized in Stockholm. The chairman was the aggressive American fighter for women's suffrage, Carrie Chapman Catt, honored as a brilliant speaker but caricatured by her opponents in newspaper cartoons as a cat surrounded by rats, symbols of male opponents of women's suffrage. The real trump card at the congress, however, was Selma Lagerlöf—Nobel Prize winner, estate owner with many employees working for her, and still a person who did not possess the elementary right to vote. Her speech, "Home and State," which she read against a background of white-clad women students, was tremendously effective. She contrasted the home—the successful creation of women—with the state—a masculine invention, marred by so many shortcomings. Her main thesis was that the participation of women is necessary if the state is to become as human as the home. She presented a vision of a more compassionate society, in which women work in mutual accord with men. Her utopian thoughts anticipated the debate of the 1970s, in which women's culture, bound up with the nurturing and preservation of life, was contrasted with the weapon technology developed by men.[25]

Lagerlöf included in "Home and State," as I have already mentioned, an interesting parallel between women's emancipation and the Swedish emigration to America. She regarded the emigration as an inevitable undertaking, a veritable force of nature, as it were. The movement of women out of the home to seek jobs and positions of responsibility was, for her, just as necessary. She envisioned a beautiful picture of the great civilizing goal of women's emancipation:

Golden wheat fields, new cities, and flourishing states show where the path of the emigrants has led. Perhaps one day, women will also prove that when they entered into the male world of work, they wanted to bring culture to the wilderness and the desert.

When women finally were given the right to vote, Lagerlöf delivered the official celebration speech, marked by Biblical phrases and high-flown hopes. For her, woman's goal was to refine humanity. Later, however, she became somewhat disappointed in the women's movement. It was difficult for her to go along with the notion of emancipation that developed during the 1920s, for she believed that the women were not as conscious of their responsibilities as they were in her youth. Privately, she did not believe that there should be limitations to occupational possibilities for women, but when she expressed herself publicly, she supported the older feminist view of women as protectors of life, preservers of peace, and bearers of culture.[26]

How is feminism reflected in Lagerlöf's texts? None of her works can be considered a direct expression of indignation. In this, Lagerlöf differs from her female predecessors in Sweden, Fredrika Bremer and Victoria Benedictsson. Yet a good deal of protest against an older patriarchal society can be seen in her literary oeuvre, in which oppression of women is a recurring theme. In *Gösta Berling's Saga*, for example, there are several variations of this theme—primarily in connection with the Major's Wife, who is forced to leave her home as a beggar because, according to the law of the day, she had no control over her own economic situation. As a young girl, she had been forced into marriage by her mother. How a girl is explicitly lured into a marriage is also the main theme of a short story, "The Riding Crop" in *Harvest*.

In many other instances, Lagerlöf has described how vulnerable and victimized women are in the role of wife and mother in older types of male societies. She takes the part of unwed mothers and sympathizes with women who seek love outside of marriage. The man as temperamental and despotic master of the family—a type that Lagerlöf had encountered in her own life—also appears in her stories.[27] Melchior Sinclaire in *Gösta Berling's Saga*, who closes his door to his own daughter; David Holm, who almost torments his wife to death in *Thy Soul Shall Bear Witness;* and Adrian Löwensköld, a man prepared to send away one of his own daughters despite his wife's deep sorrow, are examples of the same masculine ruthlessness. Another story that treats this theme is "Luftballongen" ("The Balloon"), a modern story of divorce that illustrates the weak position of the woman. The mother has left home, and she is, therefore, denied custody of her children. The father, an alcoholic with sadistic tendencies, gradually succeeds in destroying them.

Lagerlöf's fictive world, however, is not so simplified that it is always the men who are evil and the women who are good. The most purely wicked characters in her works are, indeed, women. Both Märta Dohna in *Gösta Berling's Saga* and Raklitz in *Liliecrona's Home* are clearly depicted as sadists. Thea Sundler in the Löwensköld cycle is a personification of clever calculation and helpless, distorted passion. But on the whole, Lagerlöf's women represent love and concern and a protective attitude. They are sensitive to both aesthetic and spiritual values. Her men, on the other hand, are rather often associated with militarism and crime.

The very confrontation between the masculine and the feminine lends a special dramatic tone to Lagerlöf's texts. The male characters are often used as catalysts who change the life situation of the female characters and initiate a new development in the story. This is the function, for example, of Gösta Berling, who symbolizes the erotic power so decisive for the fate of the young women in the story. The women, on the other hand, far from being passive, subordinate figures, exercise great power over the men. This can be seen in the actions of Ingrid, who in *The Tale of a Manor* stamps in anger at Gunnar Hede when he refuses to fight his illness; also, Elisabeth Dohna gives Gösta Berling a proper dressing down and speaks with great scorn about his heroism, when she wants him to return to society; and Elsalill in *The Treasure* delivers up the man she loves to be judged and sentenced.

The ability of women to influence men morally through goodness and love is a frequent theme in Lagerlöf. It appears in its pure form in works such as *Thy Soul Shall Bear Witness,* the "Legend of Saint Veronica's Veil" in *Christ Legends,* and in the short story "Mathilda Wrede" in *Trolls and Men I,* a tale based on the actual life of a Finno-Swedish woman of high birth who devoted her life to the spiritual training—and taming—of hardened criminals. With such stark contrasts between the masculine and the feminine, Lagerlöf brings into confrontation two main sides of human nature that always fascinated her: the wild, animal nature of man as opposed to the transcendental purity of the saint.

Especially in the case of women, one can discern a pattern containing mystic elements and components of the fairy tale behind her character depiction. Included in the character of the Major's Wife, for example, is a whole spectrum of archetypes—from the personification of "the beautiful soul" of Margarita Celsing to the prototypes of mother, witch, and prophetess. The role of the wicked stepmother is played by Raklitz in *Liliecrona's Home.* The roles of Cinderella and Snow White are striking in the depiction of young girls, such as Helga in "The Girl from the Marshcroft," Maja Lisa in *Liliecrona's Home,* and Ingrid in *The Tale of a Manor.* This type of woman symbolizes an inner strength not at all related to either exterior or physical power. It represents the most important moral power in existence.

The women in Lagerlöf's novels are almost always shown in relationship to their homes, families, husbands, and children. Rarely does she depict women in purely professional roles. Edith, the slum worker in *Thy Soul Shall Bear Witness,* and Sigrun, the woman who dreams of becoming a nurse in *The Outcast,* actually play the traditional role of woman as preserver of life. The Major's Wife, shown as a mother figure for an entire district, establishes a kind of matriarchy that holds the men in check, whether they be cavaliers or top representatives of society. But she must give way when the men revolt. Anna Svärd is the most clearly independent of all Lagerlöf's female characters, since she is able to support both herself and those dependent on her. There are also certain secondary characters who show Lagerlöf's interest in the working woman: the fish cleaners in *The Treasure,* the *roddarmadam,* or woman who rows boats for a living, in *The Wonderful Adventures of Nils,* and Mademoiselle Marie in *Gösta Berling's Saga,* along with a series of tersely drawn housekeepers and servant girls. The conspicuous absence of professional women is associated with the fact that Lagerlöf primarily depicts country women in a time when their roles were of great practical importance.

But that cannot be the only reason. Lagerlöf herself was, after all, an intellectual woman, long separated from the reality of the working world that she depicts in her stories. The main reason she prefers to show women in the home with their families is surely related to her own approach to human relationships and existential conditions. In order to be able to clarify them, she chose to depict real situations that most of her readers would be able to recognize. In her works, the feminist problem is integrated into the general pattern of the story; sometimes it can hardly be detected. But within this framework there is certainly far more feminist polemic than has been noted up to now.

The Myths about Selma Lagerlöf

A series of myths about Lagerlöf's role as author has been built up in Lagerlöf criticism and research and in the general consciousness as well. The label that has most often been associated with her describes her as a naive teller of tales. Using a wealth of metaphors, the leading critic in Sweden at the turn of the century, Oscar Levertin, established this image of her. Levertin wrote glowing reviews of her work in which he expressed his great admiration for her writing, but he understood her mostly as a prophetess, a seer with a mystic relationship with the very sources of myth. He believed that inspiration came to Lagerlöf in a never-ceasing stream that she could hardly keep in check.[28] This was not an accurate reflection of reality. To be sure, in certain moments of grace, Lagerlöf was able to see herself as an instrument of a higher power—her strong inspiration made her pen move by itself. But for the most part, her struggle with style and language was "difficult beyond all description."[29]

In the beginning of the 1900s, the fairy tale was held in high regard as a genre. To be regarded as a genuine teller of fairy tales was considered high praise. Lagerlöf accepted the honorary title and even called some of her stories fairy tales. But gradually the luster associated with the title "teller of fairy tales" faded, and it was not long before people began to use the less respectful name "sagotant," or "fairy-tale lady"—an appellation damaging to Lagerlöf's image.

Other features that scholars and critics often associate with Lagerlöf as an author are generally maternal feelings, mercifulness, and naiveté. The tendency among critics to apply such characteristics to her as an author led many to regard her writing primarily as too "nice" and generally unexciting; consequently readers have not become aware of the power of her imagination. They have not recognized the dark and demonic elements in her fictive world. Nor have they sufficiently regarded Lagerlöf as an analytical writer concerned with problems concealed beneath the surface of her stories.

When Elin Wägner wrote her monograph on Lagerlöf during World War II, she brought new dimensions to the official picture of Lagerlöf. Wägner sees her as a modern writer, rooted, however, in an antiquated world characterized by matriarchal elements; she points out that even the Mårbacka tradition was dominated by women. For Wägner, however, the feminine aspects of Lagerlöf's personality were not limiting; they constituted, rather, an expansive element, decisive for Lagerlöf as a writer. In contrast to many women writers, Lagerlöf did not remain in the little world; she reached out to the wide world of the epic, in which she had to wrestle with reality.

Lagerlöf possesses the art of making the reader feel that he has touched upon the very mystery of life. She seeks the most intense moments of human life, in which sloth and inactivity are overcome, and unsuspected powers come rushing forth. Fundamentally, she is one of the great worshipers of life, in which love is both star and center. But she is at the same time a strict moralist, with a strong inner sense of duty. It is precisely the confrontation between Lagerlöf the worshiper of life and Lagerlöf the moralist that causes the sparks to fly in her stories—a confrontation most fascinating in *Gösta Berling's Saga* and more tempered in the rest of her works.

With her unique mythical imagination and narrative talent, Lagerlöf cannot easily be placed into any literary-historical category. She is both a realist and a romantic. Perhaps she should be regarded primarily as a symbolist, for her work is—far more than people usually recognize—permeated with symbols. Often entire stories are illustrations of myths. Life is even "transformed into myth."[30] Nature and landscape, which in themselves are presented concretely, become the bearers of human problems and function as a parallel to them. Nature becomes identical with man, and man becomes identical with nature. This creates an interesting complexity in Lagerlöf's literary works, which, on the whole, also contain a good deal of direct conflict.

Lagerlöf's role as a storyteller has widely overshadowed her importance as a writer with humor, psychological insight, and sharp-sightedness in delineating her characters. She has created a gallery of living characters—well-rounded, believable figures. Here, too, an acute sense of human confusion and vulnerability informs her vision. Lagerlöf, who often felt herself to be cold, empty, and introverted, had the ability to hold her public spellbound with her art.

Lagerlöf's narratives, her literary language, and her mythic landscapes came to be of tremendous importance for the then impoverished Swedish prose tradition. She herself was aware of her contribution to Swedish letters. Generations of writers after her have honored her and called her their mother. Some, however, have tried to revolt against her influence, but, for the most part, they have failed. Her foremost heir in the field of prose writing is Hjalmar Bergman, who gained acclaim during the first decade of the twentieth century and, supposedly, in turn, stimulated her writing. Traces of Lagerlöf can still be seen in the wave of narratives, chronicles, and depiction of provincial life that mark Swedish literature around 1980.

Notes and References

Chapter One

1. Elin Wägner, *Selma Lagerlöf* (Stockholm: Bonnier, 1958), p. 230. Most of the biographical notes in this chapter refer to Elin Wägner's monograph.
2. Valborg Olander, *Anteckningar om Selma Lagerlöf,* manuscript in the Mårbacka collection, The Royal Library, Stockholm.
3. Ibid.
4. F. S. de Vrieze, *Fact and Fiction in the Autobiographical Works of Selma Lagerlöf* (Assen: Royal Van Gorcum, 1958). See also Eric O. Johannesson's article "Isak Dinesen and Selma Lagerlöf" in *Scandinavian Studies* 32, no. 1 (February 1960). Johannesson compares Lagerlöf's memoirs with Dinesen's *Out of Africa:* "The two books describe a lost paradise, a way of life that will never return" (p. 18).
5. Letter from Lagerlöf to Henriette Coyet dated 28 March 1932. Unless otherwise indicated, all letters written by Lagerlöf are quoted from *Selma Lagerlöfs brev,* ed. Ying Toijer-Nilsson (Stockholm: Selma Lagerlöf Society, 7, 1–2, 1967–69).
6. Ying Toijer-Nilsson, "Selma Lagerlöf–flickan som inte fann sig i sin kvinnoroll," *Lagerlöfstudier* 4 (1971).
7. Ibid.
8. Letter from Lagerlöf to Aline Laurell, 4 May 1880.
9. Wägner, *Lagerlöf,* p. 74.
10. Cf. Selma Lagerlöf, *Dockteaterspel,* ed. Ying Toijer-Nilsson (Stockholm: Selma Lagerlöf Society, 2, 1959).
11. Lagerlöf, "Två spådomar" in *Troll och människor* 2, 1921.
12. Lagerlöf, "Till Mathilda Widegren. Minnesord" in *Från skilda tider. Efterlämnade skrifter 2,* ed. Nils Afzelius (Stockholm: Bonnier, 1945). For additional comments on Lagerlöf's experiences at the teachers' training college, see Gurli Linder, "Selma-Lagerlöfsminnen," *Svensk litteraturtidskrift,* 1942.
13. Cf. Vivi Edström, "Das faustische in Gösta Berlings saga," in *Nicht nur Strindberg. Kulturelle und literarische Beziehungen zwischen Schweden und Deutschland 1870–1933,* ed. Helmut Müssener (Acta Universitatis Stockholmiensis 24, 1979), pp. 336–57.
14. Hjalmar Gullberg, *Selma Lagerlöf. Inträdestal i Svenska Akademien den 20 december 1940* (Stockholm, 1940), p. 29.
15. Letter from Lagerlöf to Sophie Adlersparre, 17 November 1891.

16. Lagerlöf, "Sophie Adlersparre," in *Höst* (Stockholm: Bonnier, 1933), p. 33.

17. Letter from Lagerlöf to Fredrika Limnell, 12 December 1891.

18. Cf. Vivi Edström, "Att framlocka det poetiskt sköna," *Lagerlöfstudier* 5 (1976).

19. Wägner, *Lagerlöf*, p. 334.

20. Jan Brunius, *Mårbacka. Gårdarnas och släkternas historia* (Stockholm: The Selma Lagerlöf Society 4, 1963), pp. 117–30.

21. Bengt Ek, *Selma Lagerlöf efter Gösta Berlings saga* (Stockholm: Bonnier, 1951), pp. 139–42. See also Olander, *Anteckningar om Selma Lagerlöf*.

22. Wägner, *Lagerlöf*, pp. 394–95.

23. Letter from Lagerlöf to Ida Bäckmann, 15 October 1933.

24. Letter from Lagerlöf to Ida Bäckmann, 22 January 1939.

Chapter Two

1. Cf. Erland Lagerroth, "Gösta Berlings saga—vår märkligaste roman?" *Lagerlöfstudier* 5 (1976):121.

2. Letter from Lagerlöf to Sophie Adlersparre, 27 April 1891.

3. Lagerroth, *Gösta,* p. 158.

4. Edström, "Att framlocka det poetiskt sköna."

5. Erland Lagerroth, *Romanen i din hand* (Stockholm: Rabén & Sjögren, 1976), p. 78.

6. Elsa Olson-Buckner, *The Epic Tradition in Gösta Berling's Saga* (New York, 1979), pp. 7, 107.

7. Alrik Gustafson, *Six Scandinavian Novelists* (Princeton, N.J.: Princeton University Press, 1971), p. 204.

8. Olson-Buckner, *Epic,* p. 59.

9. Ibid., p. 4.

10. Letter from Lagerlöf to Ida Falbe Hansen, 18 December 1891.

11. Vivi Edström, *Livets stigar. Tiden, handlingen och livskänslan i Gösta Berlings saga* (Stockholm: Svenska bokförlaget, Norstedt, 1960), p. 136.

12. Cf. Wägner, *Lagerlöf,* p. 103.

13. Cf. Letter from Lagerlöf to Sophie Adlersparre, 15 March 1891.

14. Cf. Erland Lagerroth, *Landskap och natur i Gösta Berlings saga och Nils Holgersson* (Stockholm: Bonnier, 1958), pp. 107–8.

15. Letter from Lagerlöf to Sophie Adlersparre, 15 March 1891.

16. Selma Lagerlöf, "I jättens fotspår," in *Höst* (Stockholm: Bonnier, 1933).

17. Letter from Lagerlöf to Sophie Adlersparre, 15 March 1891.

18. Edström, *Livets stigar,* p. 328.

19. Letter from Lagerlöf to Helena Nyblom, 16 January 1892.
20. Cf. Gunnar Brandell, "En liten revolution. Om verkligheten i Gösta Berlings saga," in *Revolt i dikt* (Stockholm: Bonnier/Alba, 1977), p. 36.

Chapter Three

1. See Vivi Edström, "Att finna stilen. En studie i Jerusalems framväxt," *Lagerlöfstudier* 4 (1971).
2. Regarding the factual circumstances behind Mrs. Gordon and the sea catastrophe, see Hadar Vessby, "L'Univers undergång," *Lagerlöfstudier* 3 (1966):83–109.
3. Wägner, *Lagerlöf*, pp. 164–66.
4. Hadar Vessby, "Ingmarssönerna. Bakgrund och motiv," *Lagerlöfstudier* 4 (1971):120–24.
5. Letter from Lagerlöf to Elise Malmros, 20 December 1901. On the influence of the Icelandic saga on *Jerusalem*, see Hilding Celander, "Litterära inflytelser och folklig tradition i Selma Lagerlöfs berättelser," in *Vägar till dikten* (Lund: Skrifter edition by Modersmålslärarnas förening 90, 1962). See also Nils Nihlén, "Selma Lagerlöfs *Jerusalem* och den isländska sagan," *Samlaren* 32 (1951).
6. Letter from Lagerlöf to Alfred Ipsen, 30 March 1902, in The Royal Library, Copenhagen.
7. Letter from Lagerlöf to Karl Warburg, 17 November 1903.
8. See Edström, "Att finna stilen," pp. 19, 21.
9. Sigvard Lindqvist, "Notisen som blev Ingmarssönerna," *Dagens nyheter*, 24 December 1958. See also Jan Lysén's study of *"Sons of Ingmar* as myth" in *Om Selma Lagerlöfs noveller, Lagerlöfstudier* (Stockholm: Biblioteksförlaget, 1983).
10. Letter from Lagerlöf to Karl Otto Bonnier, 29 September 1900.
11. Cf. Erland Lagerroth, *Selma Lagerlöfs Jerusalem* (Lund: Publications of the New Society of Letters, 1966), p. 11. Lagerroth stresses primarily the traditional aspects of the Ingmarssons' moral philosophy.
12. For a summing up of the discussion of Lagerlöf's divided sympathies between the emigrants and the people back home, see Lagerroth, *Selma Lagerlöfs Jerusalem*, pp. 65–71.
13. See Edström, "Att finna stilen," p. 10.
14. Vivi Edström, " 'Gud styr.' Motivförskjutningen i Jerusalem," *Lagerlöfstudier* 1 (1958):176–79.
15. Olander, *Anteckningar om Selma Lagerlöf*.
16. Ibid.
17. Cf. Edström, " 'Gud styr.' Motivförskjutningen i Jerusalem," p. 187.

Chapter Four

1. Nils Afzelius, "Sagan om Småland och sagan om det mörkaste Småland. Ett kapitel om innanläsning," in *Selma Lagerlöf—den förargelseväckande* (Stockholm: Selma Lagerlöf Society, 10, 1973), pp. 98–111.

2. Nils Afzelius, "Läsebok blir barnboksklassiker" in *Selma Lagerlöf—den förargelseväckande*, p. 87.

3. Cf. Gunnar Ahlström, *Den underbara resan. En bok om Selma Lagerlöfs Nils Holgersson* (Stockholm: Bonnier, Aldus, 1958), p. 118.

4. Cf. Ahlström, *Den underbara resan,* pp. 129–38, in which the influence of Kipling on Nils Holgersson is strongly emphasized.

5. Olander, *Anteckningar om Selma Lagerlöf.*

6. On the reception of *Nils Holgerssons underbara resa genom Sverige,* see Ahlström, pp. 49–60.

7. Ibid., p. 229.

8. Letter from Lagerlöf to Alfred Dalin, 9 May 1909.

Chapter Five

1. See Yngve Kant, "Selma Lagerlöfs noveller. En översikt" and Kant, "Lagerlöfs novellsamlingar. En kronologi," *Om Selma Lagerlöfs noveller,* Lagerlöfstudier (Stockholm: Selma Lagerlöf Society and Association of Swedish Language Teachers, Biblioteksförlaget, 1983, pp. 149–205).

2. Ek, *Selma Lagerlöf efter Gösta Berlings saga,* p. 103.

3. Ibid, pp. 124–26.

4. See Margherita Giordano Lokrantz, "Två italienska noveller av Selma Lagerlöf," *Om Selma Lagerlöfs noveller,* pp. 49–74.

5. About "The Peace of God" see Vivi Edström, "Selma Lagerlöfs Gudsfreden," *Novellanalyser,* ed. Vivi Edström and Per Arne Henricson, (Stockholm: Prisma, 1970), pp. 55–63. About "The Sons of Ingmar" see Jan Lysén, "*Ingmarssönerna* som myt," *Om Selma Lagerlöfs noveller,* pp. 93–108.

6. Cf. Ulla-Britta Lagerroth, "The Troll in Man—A Lagerlöf Motif." *Scandinavian Studies* (February 1968):51–60.

7. Hans Ritte, "Untersuchungen über die Behandlung von Volksdichtungsstoffen im Werk Selma Lagerlöfs," *Arv* 23 (1967–1968):1–94; 1–90.

8. Erik Eliasson, *Selma Lagerlöf i Landskrona* (Landskrona Musei Förening II, 1958), p. 91.

9. Nils Afzelius, "Selma Lagerlöfs 'Karln': En kommentar." *Bonniers litterära magasin,* no. 10 (1949), pp. 157–60.

10. See Karin Petherick, "Dunungen eller att finna sig själv genom kärleken," *Om Selma Lagerlöfs noveller,* pp. 11–48.

11. See Sven Arne Bergmann, "Två spelmanstexter—en konstsyn," *Om Selma Lagerlöfs noveller,* pp. 109–34.

12. Vivi Edström, *"Gravskriften—en kvinnosaksnovell?"* *Om Selma Lagerlöfs noveller,* pp. 75–92.

13. Erland Lagerroth, *Selma Lagerlöf och Bohuslän* (Stockholm: Selma Lagerlöf Society, 5, 1963), pp. 35–151.

14. Gunnel Weidel, *Helgon och gengångare. Gestaltningen av kärlek och rättvisa i Selma Lagerlöfs diktning* (Lund: Gleerup, 1964), p. 71.

15. Ibid., p. 63.

16. In conversation with the author of this study in 1954.

17. *Svenska dagbladet,* 9 December 1897.

18. Ek, *Selma Lagerlöf efter Gösta Berlings saga,* p. 100.

19. Cf. Sigvard A. Lindqvist, "Om stoff och psykologi i En herr-gårdssägen," *Lagerlöfstudier* 3 (1966):42–67, and Karin Petherick, "Hur mycket 'visste' Ingrid Berg eller den halvkvädna visan i Selma Lagerlöfs En herrgårdssägen," *Svensk Litteraturtidskrift,* no. 1 (1981), pp. 37–47.

20. Nils Afzelius, "Herr Arnes penningar varar ännu" in *Selma Lagerlöf—den förargelseväckande,* pp. 58–64.

21. Gösta Werner, *Herr Arnes pengar. En filmvetenskaplig studie och dokumentation av Mauritz Stillers film efter Selma Lagerlöfs berättelse* (Stockholm: Norstedt, 1979).

22. Weidel, *Helgon och gengångare,* pp. 247–61.

23. Ibid., pp. 232–33. See also Louise Winge, "Vad händer i Herr Arnes penningar?" *Lagerlöfstudier* (Stockholm: Selma Lagerlöf Society, 3, 1966), pp. 110–25.

24. Cheri Register, "Herr Arnes penningar som feministisk myt," *Ord och bild,* no 6 (1979):27–37.

Chapter Six

1. Ulla-Britta Lagerroth, *Körkarlen och Bannlyst. Motiv-och idéstudier i Selma Lagerlöfs 10-talsdiktning* (Stockholm: Bonnier, 1963), p. 25.

2. About the sources of inspiration for *Körkarlen,* see Ulla-Britta Lagerroth, pp. 132–37.

3. See Gardar Sahlberg, "Selma Lagerlöf och filmen," *Lagerlöfstudier* 2 (1961):199, 205.

4. Letter from Lagerlöf to Ida Falbe Hansen, 11 January 1913.

5. Alrik Gustafson, *A History of Swedish Literature* (Minneapolis: University of Minnesota Press for the American Scandinavian Foundation, 1961), p. 314.

6. Letter from Lagerlöf to Emilia (Mim) Rydberg, 18 September 1886.

7. Ulla-Britta Lagerroth, *Körkarlen,* pp. 175–77.

8. Kjell Wallström, "Kärlekens skapande kraft i Kejsarn av Portugallien," *Lagerlöfstudier* 5 (1976):44.

9. Letter from Lagerlöf to Karl Otto Bonnier, 4 September 1914.
10. Wallström, "Karlekens," pp. 65–85.
11. Cf. Margherita Giordano Lokrantz, "Två italienska noveller av Selma Lagerlöf," *Lagerlöfstudier*, 1983, pp. 49–65.
12. Wägner, *Lagerlöf*, p. 281.
13. Ulla-Britta Lagerroth, *Körkarlen*, p. 378.
14. Ibid., p. 374.
15. Letter from Lagerlöf to Kajsa Hansen, 5 April 1919.

Chapter Seven

1. Selma Lagerlöf, *Ett barns memoarer (Memories of My Childhood)* (Stockholm: Bonnier, 1930), p. 189.
2. Lars Ulvenstam, *Den åldrade Selma Lagerlöf* (Stockholm: Bonnier, 1955), p. 141.
3. Wägner, *Lagerlöf*, p. 336.
4. Letter from Lagerlöf to Elisabeth Grundvig, 12 November 1925.
5. Ulvenstam, *Den åldrade*, pp. 84–95.
6. Letter from Lagerlöf to Elin Lagerlöf, 16 October 1924.

Chapter Eight

1. Letter from Lagerlöf to Stella Rydholm, 2 January 1924.
2. Letter from Lagerlöf to Hellen Lindgren, 25 October 1902.
3. Wägner, *Lagerlöf*, p. 351.
4. Oscar Levertin and Verner von Heidenstam, *Pepitas bröllop. En litteraturanmälan.* (Stockholm, 1890), pp. 37, 39.
5. Quoted from Wilhelm Söderhjelm, *Oscar Levertin* 1 (Stockholm: Bonnier, 1914), p. 306.
6. Weidel, *Helgon,* pp. 39–45.
7. Gunnar Ahlström, *Kring Gösta Berlings saga* (Stockholm: Natur och kultur, 1959), p. 31.
8. Letter from Lagerlöf to Sophie Adlersparre, 14 April 1891.
9. Letter from Lagerlöf to Fredrika Limnell, 12 December 1891.
10. Letter from Lagerlöf to Eva Fryxell, 10 February 1892.
11. Letter from Lagerlöf to Sophie Adlersparre, 29 November 1891.
12. Letter from Lagerlöf to Eva Fryxell, 10 February 1892.
13. Lagerlöf, "Vädjan till Amerika," in *Från skilda tider* 2.
14. Afzelius, "Herr Arnes penningar varar ännu," in *Selma Lagerlöf—den förargelseväckande,* p. 58.
15. Jacob Kulling, *Huvudgestalten i Selma Lagerlöfs författarskap* (Stockholm: Svenska kyrkans diakonistyrelses förlag, 1959). Cf. letters from Lagerlöf to Henriette Coyet, 16 March and 27 April 1930, where she discusses her relation to Christianity.

16. Erland Lagerroth, "The Narrative Art of Selma Lagerlöf," *Scandinavian Studies* 33, no. 1 (February 1961):15.

17. Erland Lagerroth, "Att låta många stämmor tala," *Lagerlöfstudier* 6 (1979):60–74.

18. Daniel Popp and E. C. Barksdale, "Selma Lagerlöf: The Taleteller's Fugues," *Scandinavian Studies* 53, no. 4 (Autumn 1981): "Many of the characteristic features of her style, her unusual plots, themes, and stylistic effects can be better understood by studying the ways in which she treated folklore" (p. 405).

19. Letter from Lagerlöf to Stella Rydholm, 22 October 1921.

20. Letter from Lagerlöf to Elisabeth Grundtvig, 23 December 1913.

21. Wägner, *Lagerlöf,* p. 281.

22. Letter from Lagerlöf to Fredrik Ström, 14 December 1903.

23. Stellan Arvidson, *Selma Lagerlöf* (Stockholm: Bonnier, 1932), p. 134.

24. Letter from Lagerlöf to Ida Bäckmann, 10 October 1913.

25. Edström, "Selma Lagerlöf och kvinnans röstratt," *Lagerlöfstudier* 6 (1979):27–59.

26. Ibid.

27. Ibid.

28. Oscar Levertin, "Selma Lagerlöf," in *Svenska gestalter* (Stockholm: Bonnier, 1903), p. 284.

29. Letter from Lagerlöf to Helena Nyblom, 25 May 1891.

30. Johannesson, *Scandinavian Studies* 1 (1960):22.

Selected Bibliography

PRIMARY SOURCES

1. First Editions

Gösta Berlings saga. Stockholm: Fritiof Hellberg, 1891. Later editions edited by Bonnier, Stockholm.

Osynliga länkar. Stockholm: Bonnier, 1894.

Antikrists mirakler. Stockholm: Bonnier, 1897.

Drottningar i Kungahälla jämte andra berättelser, Stockholm: Bonnier, 1897.

En herrgårdssägen. Stockholm: Bonnier, 1899.

Jerusalem 1. I Dalarne. Stockholm: Bonnier, 1901.

Jerusalem 2. I det heliga landet. Stockholm: Bonnier, 1902.

Herr Arnes penningar. Stockholm: Iduns red. 1903.

Kristuslegender. Stockholm: Bonnier, 1904.

Nils Holgersson 1. Stockholm: Bonnier, 1906.

Nils Holgersson 2. Stockholm: Bonnier, 1907.

En saga om en saga och andra sagor. Stockholm: Bonnier, 1908.

Liljecronas hem. Stockholm: Bonnier, 1911.

Hem och stat. Föredrag vid Rösträttskongressen den 13 juni 1911. Stockholm: Bonnier, 1911.

Körkarlen. Stockholm: Bonnier, 1912.

Kejsarn av Portugallien. Stockholm: Bonnier, 1914.

Troll och människor. Stockholm: Bonnier, 1915.

Bannlyst. Stockholm: Bonnier, 1918.

Zachris Topelius. Utveckling och mognad. Stockholm: Bonnier, 1920.

Troll och människor 2. Stockholm: Bonnier, 1921.

Mårbacka. Stockholm: Bonnier, 1922.

Löwensköldska ringen. Stockholm: Bonnier, 1925.

Charlotte Löwensköld. Stockholm: Bonnier, 1925.

Anna Svärd. Stockholm: Bonnier, 1928.

Mårbacka 2. Ett barns memoarer. Stockholm: Bonnier, 1930.

Mårbacka 3. Dagbok. Stockholm: Bonnier, 1932.

Höst. Berättelser och tal. Stockholm: Bonnier, 1933.

Skrifter 1933. Many later printings and editions.

Från skilda tider. Efterlämnade skrifter 1. Edited by Nils Afzelius. Stockholm: Bonnier, 1943.

Från skilda tider. Efterlämnade skrifter 2. Edited by Nils Afzelius. Stockholm: Bonnier, 1945.

2. English Translations

Charlotte Löwensköld. Translated by Velma Swanston Howard. Garden City, N.Y.: Doubleday, 1927.

Christ Legends. Translated by Velma Swanston Howard. New York: Holt, Rinehart & Winston, 1908, and later editions.

The Diary of Selma Lagerlöf. Translated by Velma Swanston Howard. Garden City, N.Y.: Doubleday, 1936.

The Emperor of Portugallia. Translated by Velma Swanston Howard. Garden City, N.Y.: Doubleday, 1917.

Further Adventures of Nils. Translated by Velma Swanston Howard. Garden City, N.Y.: Doubleday, 1911, and later editions.

The General's Ring. Translated by Francesca Martin. Garden City, N.Y.: Doubleday, 1928.

The Girl From the Marshcroft. Translated by Velma Swanston Howard. Boston: Little, Brown, 1910; Garden City, N.Y.: Doubleday, 1916, 1924.

Gösta Berling's Saga. Translated by Lillie Tudeer. London: 1898. Translated by Velma Swanston Howard. New York: American-Scandinavian Foundation, 1918. New editions translated by Lillie Tudeer and Velma S. Howard. New York: 1928, 1960.

Harvest. Translated by Florence and Naboth Hedin. Garden City, N.Y.: Doubleday, Doran, 1935.

The Holy City—Jerusalem II. Translated by Velma Swanston Howard. Garden City, N.Y.: Doubleday, 1918.

Invisible Links. Translated by Pauline Bancroft Flach. Boston: Little, Brown, 1899; later editions 1909, 1912, 1918.

Jerusalem. Translated by Velma Swanston Howard. Garden City, N.Y.: Doubleday, 1915, and later editions.

Liliecrona's Home. Translated by Anna Barwell. New York: E. P. Dutton, 1914.

Memories of My Childhood: Further Years at Mårbacka. Translated by Velma Swanston Howard. Garden City, N.Y.: Doubleday, Doran, 1934.

The Miracles of Antichrist. Translated by Pauline B. Flach. Boston: Little, Brown, 1910. Another English rendering of this novel is by Selma Ahlström Trotz. New York: Lovell, 1899.

Mårbacka. Translated by Velma Swanston Howard. Garden City, N.Y.: Doubleday, 1922.

The Outcast. Translated by W. Worster. Garden City, N.Y.: Doubleday, 1922.

Queens of Kungahälla and Other Sketches. Translated by C. Field. London: T. W. Laurie, 1930.

The Ring of the Löwensfölds. Translated by Francesca Martin and Velma
Swanston Howard. Garden City, N.Y.: Doubleday, Doran, 1931. A
trilogy including *The General's Ring, Charlotte Löwensköld,* and *Anna
Svärd.*
The Story of Gösta Berling. Translated by Pauline Bancroft Flach. Boston:
Little, Brown, 1898, and many later editions.
The Story of Gösta Berling. Translated with an afterword by Robert Bly.
New York: New American Library (Signet Classic), 1962. Reprinted
in Karlstad: Press Förlag, 1982.
The Tale of a Manor. Translated by C. Field. London: T. W. Laurie, 1923.
Thy Soul Shall Bear Witness. Translated by W. F. Harvey. London: Odhams
Press, 1921.
The Treasure. Translated by Arthur G. Chater. Garden City, N.Y.: Dou-
bleday, Page, 1925.
The Wonderful Adventure of Nils. Translated by Velma Swanston Howard.
Garden City, N.Y.: Doubleday, 1907. Frequently reissued, often in
illustrated editions. New York: Pantheon, 1947.
The Wonderful Adventures of Nils. Translated by Richard E. Oldenburg.
Garden City, N.Y.: Doubleday, 1967.

SECONDARY SOURCES

Afzelius, Nils. *Selma Lagerlöf—den förargelseväckande.* Stockholm: Selma
Lagerlöf Society, 10, 1973.
Ahlström, Gunnar. *Den underbara resan. En bok om Selma Lagerlöfs Nils
Holgersson.* Stockholm: Bonnier/Aldus, 1958.
———. *Kring Gösta Berlings saga.* Stockholm: Natur och kultur, 1959.
Berendsohn, Walter A. *Selma Lagerlöf. Heimat und Leben.* Münich: Albert
Langen, 1927.
———. *Selma Lagerlöf. Her Life and Work.* Adapted from the German by
George F. Timpson. Port Washington, N.Y.: Kennikat Press, 1968.
de Vrieze, F. S. *Fact and Fiction in the Autobiographical Works of Selma
Lagerlöf.* Assen: Royal Van Gorcum, 1958.
Edström, Vivi. "Att finna stilen. En studie i Jerusalems framväxt." *Lag-
erlöfstudier* 4 (1971):7–32.
———. "Att framlocka det poetiskt sköna. Selma Lagerlöfs revolt mot
80-talsrealismen." *Lagerlöfstudier* 5 (1976):91–119.
———. "Das faustische in Gösta Berlings Saga." In *Nicht nur Strindberg.
Kulturelle und literarische Beziehungen zwischen Schweden und Deutschland
1870–1933.* Edited by Helmut Müssener. Acta Universitatis Stock-
holmiensis 24, 1979, pp. 336–57.

Selected Bibliography 145

---. "Gud styr. Motivförskjutningen i Jerusalem." *Lagerlöfstudier* 1 (1958):157–87.

---. *Livets stigar. Tiden, handlingen och livskänslan i Gösta Berlings saga.* Stockholm: Svenska bokförlaget, Norstedt, 1960.

---. "Selma Lagerlöf och kvinnans röstratt." *Lagerlöfstudier* 6 (1979):27–59.

Ek, Bengt. *Selma Lagerlöf efter Gösta Berlings saga.* Stockholm: Bonnier, 1951.

Gustafson, Alrik. *A History of Swedish Literature.* Minneapolis: University of Minnesota Press for the American Scandinavian Foundation, 1961.

---. *Six Scandinavian Novelists.* Princeton, N.J.: Princeton University Press, 1971.

Johannesson, Eric O. "Isak Dinesen and Selma Lagerlöf." *Scandinavian Studies* 32, no. 1 (February 1960):18–26.

Lagerlöfstudier. Stockholm: Selma Lagerlöf Society: 1958, 1961, 1966, 1971, 1976, 1979, 1983.

Lagerroth, Erland. "Att låta många stämmor tala," *Lagerlöfstudier* 6 (1979):60–74.

---. "Gösta Berlings saga—vår märkligaste roman?" *Lagerlöfstudier* 5 (1976):121–62.

---. *Landskap och natur i Gösta Berlings saga och Nils Holgersson.* Stockholm: Bonnier, 1958.

---. "The Narrative Art of Selma Lagerlöf. Two Problems." *Scandinavian Studies* 33, no. 1 (February 1961):10–17.

---. *Selma Lagerlöf och Bohuslän.* Stockholm: Selma Lagerlöf Society, 5, 1963.

---. *Selma Lagerlöfs Jerusalem.* Publications of the New Society of Letters, Lund: 1966.

Lagerroth, Ulla-Britta. *Körkarlen och Bannlyst. Motiv-och idéstudier i Selma Lagerlöfs 10-talsdiktning.* Stockholm: Bonnier, 1963.

---. "The Troll in Man—A Lagerlöf Motif." *Scandinavian Studies* 40, no. 1 (February 1968):51–60.

Lindqvist, Sigvard A. "Om stoff och psykologi i En herrgårdssägen." *Lagerlöfstudier* 3 (1966):42–67.

Olson-Buckner, Elsa. *The Epic Tradition in Gösta Berling's Saga.* New York: Theo. Gans, 1979.

Om Selma Lagerlöfs noveller. Lagerlöfstudier. Stockholm: Biblioteksförlaget, 1983.

Petherick, Karin. "Hur mycket 'visste' Ingrid Berg eller den halvkvädna visan i Selma Lagerlöfs En herrgårdssägen." *Svensk litteraturtidskrift,* no. 1 (1981), pp. 37–47.

Popp, Daniel, and Barksdale, E.C. "Selma Lagerlöf: The Taleteller's Fugues." *Scandinavian Studies* 53, no. 4 (Autumn 1981):405–12.

Register, Cheri. "Herr Arnes penningar som feministisk myt." *Ord och bild,* no. 6 (1979), pp. 27–37.

Ritte, Hans. "Untersuchungen über die Behandling von Volksdichtungs-stoffen im Werk Selma Lagerlöfs." *Arv,* 1967–68, pp. 1–94, 1–90.

Toijer-Nilsson, Ying. Introduction to Selma Lagerlöf, *Dockteaterspel.*

————. "Naturens förbannelse. En studie i Selma Lagerlöfs naturuppfattning." *Samlaren,* 1954, pp. 169–213.

————. "Selma Lagerlöf—flickan som inte fann sig i sin kvinnoroll." *Lagerlöfstudier* 4 (1971):46–63.

Ulvenstam, Lars. *Den åldrade Selma Lagerlöf.* Stockholm: Bonnier, 1955.

Vessby, Hadar. "L'Univers undergång." *Lagerlöfstudier* 3 (1966):83–109.

————, "Ingmarssönerna. Bakgrund och motiv." *Lagerlöfstudier* 4 (1971):116–47.

Wägner, Elin. *Selma Lagerlöf.* Stockholm: Bonnier, 1958.

Wallström, Kjell. "Kärlekens skapande kraft i Kejsarn av Portugallien." Lagerlöfstudier 5 (1976):41–90.

Weidel, Gunnel. *Helgon och gengångare. Gestaltningen av kärlek och rättvisa i Selma Lagerlöfs diktning.* Lund: Gleerup, 1964.

Werner, Gösta. *Herr Arnes pengar. En filmvetenskaplig studie och dokumentation av Mauritz Stillers film efter Selma Lagerlöfs berättelse.* Stockholm: Norstedt, 1979.

Winge, Louise. "Vad händer i Herr Arnes penningar?" *Lagerlöfstudier* 3 (1966):110–25.

Index

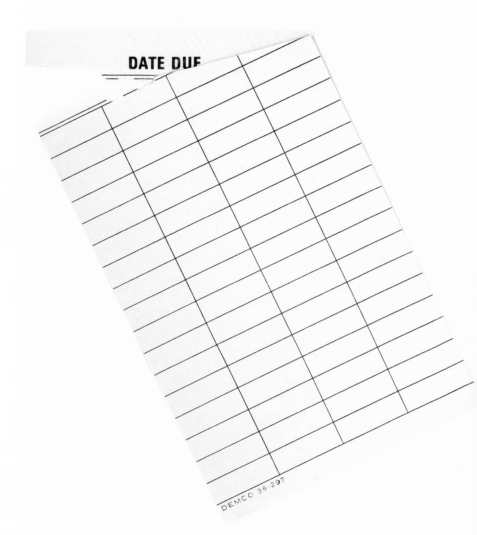

DATE DUE

DEMCO 38-297